WHAT PEOPLE ARE SAYING ABOUT

HOLDING OUT FOR A HERO

Heartfelt and thorough, hor   on Botez's *Holding Out For A Her*   ɔle guide to romance over forty. Lesley is a great guide and this is a charming handbook.

Jonathan Barnes, author of *The Somnambulist* and *The Domino Men*

As Pastor of the Emmanuel Church, serving the expatriate and local communities in Geneva, I am pleased to see the publication of *Holding Out for a Hero*. It is not only well but also wisely written. Through her own intimate story and those of the other couples interviewed, Lesley has provided timely and practical guidance for those who seek to find their own hero or heroine later in life. Her various case studies testify to the fact that love is more powerful than anxiety and fear.

The Rev. John Beach, Emmanuel Church, Geneva

There's a conversational style and humane approach throughout which seems both practical and encouraging without being patronizing.

Siobhan Campbell, author and critic, Associate Professor at Kingston University London

Lesley Lawson Botez is committed to preparing couples well for marriage and using FOCCUS. In her book she explores the relevance of marriage preparation and the importance of asking the right questions, communicated properly, early on in the relationship.

Valerie H. Conzett, D. Min., L.P.C., Executive Director, FOCCUS, Inc. USA

Holding out for a Hero is accessible to a wide variety of readers, both men and women. It contains examples and case studies that are thought provoking.

All in all the book reminds us that there is always hope, but that we need to be open and willing to recognize it.

Dr Sigrid Newman, University of Cologne

A delightful read, full of charming anecdotes, subtle British humour, and much straightforward good advice. "Enjoy the experience," writes the author. I certainly did.

Peter St John, author of the "Gang" series

Lesley Lawson Botez has written an excellent book about marriage over 40. By deftly combining her personal experience with the experience of countless others, along with relevant exercises, she has created an informed guidebook not only to marriage over 40 but also to romance over forty. Her own love story is a delight to read. The proposed path, with five steps, is traced with her professional hand as a psychologist. And the whole is written with fine craft, humor and love.

Susan Tiberghien, author of *Looking for Gold, A Year in Jungian Analysis*, and *One Year to a Writing Life*

Holding Out for a Hero

Five Steps to Marriage over 40

Holding Out for a Hero

Five Steps to Marriage over 40

Lesley Lawson Botez

Winchester, UK
Washington, USA

First published by Bedroom Books, 2014
Bedroom Books is an imprint of John Hunt Publishing Ltd., Laurel House, Station Approach,
Alresford, Hants, SO24 9JH, UK
office1@jhpbooks.net
www.johnhuntpublishing.com
www.bedroom-books.com

For distributor details and how to order please visit the 'Ordering' section on our website.

Text copyright: Lesley Lawson Botez 2014

ISBN: 978 1 78279 514 8

A CIP catalogue record for this book is available from the British Library.

Design: Lee Nash

Printed in the USA by Edwards Brothers Malloy

We operate a distinctive and ethical publishing philosophy in all
areas of our business, from our global network of authors to
production and worldwide distribution.

CONTENTS

For the singles who will read this book. I hope you find what you are looking for.

Acknowledgements

The origins of this book come from my interest, as a psychologist and newly-wed, in finding out how others were experiencing first time marriage in their 40s and 50s.

Many wonderful people from the US, Europe and Australia answered my survey through writers' groups, marriage sites, expatriate groups and my own website. They agreed to be interviewed openly and honestly. To protect their identities, I have changed places and names but thank all of them for participating with enthusiasm and openness.

The Geneva Writers' Group has been a source of support and encouragement since the anonymous reading of the first page of my manuscript at the 2011 "Meet the Agents" conference. In particular, GWG director Susan Tiberghien has been an inspiration. Writers Marianne Bertsch-Junger, Jo Anne Rausch and Caroline Thonger have shared their ideas generously. Writer Natasha Scott gave me new insights and challenged my perspective through her critiquing. The incredibly talented La Forge literary group of Ginny, Peter, Rosalind, Karin, Leslie, Jule, Chamouni, Emanita, Martha, Sally and Sanda have given invaluable feedback as I progressed through the Steps.

Writers from the Swanwick Writers' School have followed the development of this book since I first attended in 2011 and had the honour of teaching in 2012.

Thanks to author and lecturer, Jonathan Barnes at Kingston University who has kept me focussed throughout, in particular with the more sensitive sections of the book.

Thanks to the real Late Bloomer Bride, Suzanne Henry, who has encouraged and supported me from the beginning.

My Cyprus Poodle Vinnie has been a patient listener as I read my chapters to him. He must have taken good note as he has now found two partners: one online and one in the park.

Most important, thanks to my own Hero, my husband David, who has encouraged me through the process of researching, writing and producing this book. We have discussed issues, including painful ones, over a glass of Chardonnay, in a spirit of truth and honesty. Your skills with tricky layouts are unsurpassed. Believe me, it was worth holding out for a Hero.

Introduction

How this book can help you

Holding Out for a Hero is inspired by my own first time marriage in my 40s. Friends and acquaintances remarked on the change in me, how I radiated happiness. After years of ups and downs, I had found relationship stability. Looking around me, newly married friends of my age all appeared delighted with their new status, often to their surprise. We had spent years avoiding settling down, perhaps through studying, building our careers, travelling or simply because we weren't ready. Now here we were, lapping up life as part of a couple.

Not that everyone who says that they want to marry and didn't when they were young does so at 40+. In the UK, there are 15 million singles between the ages of 18 and 65. Over half this number claim to be looking for a meaningful relationship and yet don't seem to be finding it. Could the insights of newly-weds in their 40s and beyond be helpful to singles who were still looking? Calling upon my training and experience as a psychologist, I began my research.

One of my first discoveries was that many who marry over 40 for the first time have relocated within their own country or elsewhere. Some are expatriates or humanitarian workers. The Rector of Emmanuel Church in Geneva, my town of adoption with a significant ex-pat community, told me that the average age of newly-weds in his church was 42. Although he couldn't specify whether it was a first or later marriage, it is still significant.

To draw wider conclusions, I looked beyond Geneva. I contacted writers' groups elsewhere in Europe, expatriate associations and marriage sites in Europe and the US. I put a survey on my website.

Masses of inspiring stories from over 40s came in from all

over the Western world. Each told of new beginnings; challenges faced and love conquered. All had in common a new awareness, a dramatic shift in perception that had led to a change in behaviour. This change had attracted love into their lives.

I analysed these case histories to understand what had gone right in order to share them with you, the reader. The stories and my findings form the basis of this book. They will help you to gain a new perspective of your own situation.

Why marriage, you might ask, rather than just living together? Marriage is a benchmark to evaluate the stage of commitment in a relationship. The role of the institution has changed dramatically in the last 50 years. The rapid growth in later and same sex marriages shows that its purpose is no longer primarily as a base for bringing up a family. On the other hand, while the rigid rules and regulations of previous generations are no longer adhered to, our expectations have risen. We enter into marriage freely as a rule. It has evolved into a partnership that provides a safe haven in a changing world.

Keeping love over 40 is as important as finding it.

How to use this book

If you want a relationship that will bring you happiness and stability without giving up your true self, working through the Steps in this book will increase the likelihood of your finding it.

Part I of *Holding out for a Hero* tells of my personal journey from single to married. It relates the quest that I undertook to find love after 40 years in the desert, and the rocks and dunes that I encountered on the way. When I met my hero, David, there were still more rocks to clamber over, challenges that I faced at over 40 in a quite different way to a 25 year old. What I had imagined being a year of balmy happiness was full of ups and downs. David and I came through them together, the bond between us stronger from all that had happened.

If you are impatient to get going on your own journey, you might want to leave this section till later although it has lessons to be shared.

Part II is your story, a journey of self-discovery from single to married if that is what you decide. Like a fairy tale, Step One begins with you, at home. Although you probably have a good job, friends and a comfortable home, you are not totally happy. At 40+, you feel that something or rather someone is missing from your otherwise satisfactory existence: a partner. You hear The Call and decide it is time for change. You pick up this book; your journey has begun. Through specific exercises and examples you take a fresh look at internal obstacles that could be blocking your path to happiness and see how to dismantle them.

In Step Two, you are ready to go out into the world and test your new knowledge and perspective. You will learn about the best places to meet a partner and do some exercises to help you on your way. You may well have an initial success and meet someone new. You will look at whether this is the right person for you in Step Three.

If you have met a potential partner and are wondering if it could lead to something serious, you could go directly to Step Three and read on from there. You might even like to do some of the exercises with your partner. This step is called the Central Crisis because it is here that a lot of your decision taking will be done. You will see whether this was just a false start or if it could become a happy ending.

Step Four presents you with some final hurdles to get over, such as past baggage, children and sharing your space. These are sensitive issues that often come up. In Step Five, the Final Union and Fulfilment, you emerge victoriously and lay claim to your kingdom, if you so wish.

Although your quest for a loving relationship is an individual one, you are not alone. Many men and women have been where you are now and found love. Their stories will accompany and inspire you throughout the book. Your journey will be different to theirs, but it is a journey that you have chosen yourself, and that is what makes it special.

Enjoy the experience.

Part I

Countdown to the Wedding

Countdown to the Wedding

I always knew that I'd marry one day. I just hoped it wouldn't be too soon. Countless astrologers had assured me that it was written in the stars, but not now. For me, next year was soon enough. Yet as the big four O came and went I wondered if I were doing something wrong. I held a high-powered job, had great legs and led a reasonable social life, albeit often with other single women. So what was holding me back?

A clue lay in my choice of partners. I chose so unwisely so often that it couldn't be a coincidence. Take the handsome 40-year-old lawyer who claimed to be single because he had not yet found the woman of his dreams. In fact, he had a wife in the US, an eight-month pregnant girlfriend in Zurich and me. I learnt about these rivals during a moonlight ski expedition. I drunkenly descended the slopes on the shoulders of an ex-lover who happened to be there. We won first prize proving the adage about unlucky in love.

Perhaps the most revealing event happened long before I was 40, on my 32nd birthday. I was engaged for the third time and received a dozen long-stemmed roses from my fiancé, conveniently on a business trip to Australia. Yes, that was the ski champion with the broad shoulders I mentioned just now. I realized how much easier it was to dream of him at a distance than to put up with his going skiing at 8 a.m. every winter weekend. I wanted to stay in bed and cuddle.

Timetable inconsistencies weren't the only indication of our incompatibility. My fiancé organised a celebratory engagement party in a famous London Oyster Bar, without me. When I received a compassionate letter from his mother advising me to enjoy the engagement months, as they would be the happiest of my life, I decided to call it off.

In between and often during these lopsided relationships,

there were the lonely, post-party taxis home and the Saturday night video dates with my Yorkshire terrier, Bumble.

I made it harder to meet someone by choosing Geneva as a home base, a city notorious for its Calvinistic coolness and lack of men. There is one eligible man to eight women by some counts. Not that it is any easier for men. Finding someone with the same sense of humour and shared values is difficult at the best of times, even more so when you are over 40. In a transient society where everyone is on the move it becomes a challenge.

All was well professionally but not great romantically. My career was my driving force. I had run my own communications agency before being asked to set up the communications department of a private banking group. I soon found that banking was not for me and took a completely different direction by moving to the International Committee of the Red Cross. I was responsible for publications produced worldwide and travelled extensively.

My life, though outwardly cushy, was lonely. I didn't enjoy being alone, but I seemed powerless to change it. I was too frightened of being vulnerable, caught in a relationship where I could be let down at any minute. Better to live in my dreams of meeting Mr Perfect or hang out with Mr Very Unperfect than risk pain and suffering with Mr Possible Potential.

I realized I needed to do something drastic to break with the past and celebrate the upcoming birthday at the same time. It was Bob, an intrepid traveller and banker friend, who told me about a study tour following in the footsteps of Moses through five deserts in the Middle East. It was to be a journey of spiritual awakening organised by the Rector of Geneva's Emmanuel Church. The participants would spend two weeks sleeping in the open air on freezing November nights, eating round a campfire, washing their hands in the sand, and peeing in the open air, the men's wadi to the right, the women's to the left. It sounded perfect. Forgetting that I had never even been on a Brownie camping trip, I was swayed by the idea of seeing shooting stars and making wishes. I liked the symbolism of emerging after 40 years in the desert.

It was time to break up with Lars. He was Scandinavian; I had known him since we had boarded at neighbouring schools. We had been seeing each other for about six months. I could count on him to come round with a hammer to put up pictures in my new flat. He would also pick me up at the airport when I returned from places like Sarajevo.

"There are 14 people waiting to have dinner with you and learn about your trip," he'd say. I appreciated how he'd organised all these new people for me to meet. I just wished he'd realized that I'd been in a city where water was rationed, and baths could only be taken three afternoons a week. I was tired and stinky and not in the mood for dinner parties. When he asked if we could split the bill – he'd lost all his money in a dicey deal in Siberia – I knew this would not do.

"You might meet your Prince in the desert," predicted Ilona, a farsighted single friend, as I prepared for the trip.

"What, on a church trip?" I asked, although her remark reflected the answer the runes had given me two weeks before.

To my usual question "Will I meet someone soon?" they had replied, "Yes, in two to three weeks and it will be serious."

I immediately bought a tombola ticket on the strength of their response. Good luck comes in series; I won third prize, a beautiful 19th century etching of Naples that I treasure to this day. With Ilona and the runes in mind, I set off on 13 November.

First stop

On the plane, I was seated next to David. I had seen him at the orientation session, but we had not talked. We were in row 11 on an Austrian Airlines flight from Geneva to Vienna where we would change for Tel Aviv. He was in his early 50s with grey curly hair and horn-rimmed glasses. I liked his American square-jawed looks, his generous smile and the way he peered over his glasses to read. Only his rust-coloured suede jacket was not to my taste. Not that I was dressed to kill exactly. I had on large shapeless trousers and a billowing top. I had replaced my contact lenses with wire-rimmed Armani glasses. I looked like a swot.

David's laptop was open on the table. Engrossed in his work, he spent the first part of the trip tapping away with pianist's fingers on the keyboard. His nails were chewed to the quick.

When the stewardess came round with the drinks, I asked for a mineral water in Goethe Institute German.

My neighbour looked up, "I'll have the same." We began to chat. He had been on a similar Middle East trip 12 years before.

"It gives you time to think, take decisions," he assured me. "We sleep under the stars and there are no telephones, computers or other interruptions."

That was exactly what I was looking for. I was fed up with more than just the situation with Lars. The professional and social limitations of small town Geneva were wearing me down. I wanted to move back to London and had applied for Swiss nationality so that I would retain the right to return to Geneva if things didn't work out.

For some reason, I had an urge to tell this charming stranger beside me about my birthday. I had not told anyone up until then.

"Which day next week?" he asked.

"Wednesday," I said.

"Wednesday? That's my birthday too."

I was flabbergasted; that was the last thing that I had expected to hear. How often does that happen? I've known people with birthdays on 16, 17, 18 and 20 November. But the very same day as me? That was a coincidence. I knew I'd have ample opportunity to check his passport for confirmation as we crisscrossed over the borders of Israel, Egypt and Jordan.

"Wow, that's amazing. I know that there are famous people with the same birthday as me like Meg Ryan, Jodi Foster and Larry King, but I've never met anyone born the same day before."

"Don't forget James A. Garfield, the 20th President of the United States. He was in office for less than a year before the assassination attempt that left him badly injured. It wasn't the assassin that killed him, but the hospital."

"I can't say I've ever heard of James A. Garfield."

"Well, there you are, same birthday as you and me. By the way I hope you brought a bottle of champagne to make a toast. I've got my bottle in my knapsack."

"No, I didn't bring champagne. I wasn't sure that I wanted to mention my birthday. After all, I don't know anyone here apart from Bob."

"Not mention it? Of course you have to mention it. It's your day to celebrate. I'm sure that you can get a bottle in Vienna when we change planes."

It was settled. In Vienna, I bought champagne while David grabbed his mobile phone and called the office.

On the next flight, I learnt more about him. He had married three times, and yet he seemed so gentle and reassuring. For some reason, I associated serial husbands with brash behaviour. Not that his many marriages bothered me, my mother had been a fourth wife, my sister a third wife, and my friends at boarding school in Lausanne had multiple stepparents whose names and birthdays they had difficulty remembering.

Then there was David's girlfriend Doris, a childhood sweetheart. She had popped up a year before, getting his address from his mother in Virginia. They had not met in 33 years. He had invited her on the trip but at the last moment she had cancelled. One of her sons was in trouble, and she had to bale him out. David had forfeited the money for her trip, and the place had been offered to someone else, at his expense.

"It's a shame, isn't it?" He looked saddened by her absence but not devastated.

Then he told me about his children; a son of 24 in the States and an eight-year-old daughter in Switzerland. Thinking about it

I did remember the daughter from the orientation session. She had appeared to me as a mass of blonde hair and bows dressed in lilac pyjamas. I was struck by how he seemed to get as much support from putting his arm on her shoulders as she got protection from him.

Professionally he ran an international law practice. He entertained me with tales of the lex loci delicti or law of the place of the fault, his speciality. I racked my brain to think how I could return the favour with International Humanitarian Law.

In Jerusalem that evening we found ourselves alone again, together for a drink on a terrace overlooking the Holy City. We were the only customers. The atmosphere was hushed, unsettling. I had a feeling something was in preparation that we did not know about. We ordered local Emerald wine. I noticed how quickly David consumed three glasses while I sipped one till it got warm. I plied him with questions about his birth chart, keen to know his ascendant and other planetary particulars. His most recent ex-wife, also a Scorpio, had had his chart drawn up, and he would have to check with her. Back at our 19th century pilgrims' palace hotel, he surprised me with a kiss on the cheek. I had enjoyed his company over drinks, but I felt him to be fragile. I was not convinced that the absence of his returning teenage sweetheart was the cause.

A night under the stars

We left Jerusalem for the wilds of the Negev Desert. I didn't sleep much that first night in the open air. I was far too excited. It was colder than I had imagined. The space was immense. In spite of the shuddering snores from some of my male companions, I felt like I was alone in the wilderness, close to the absolute. I was wrapped in borrowed British Airways First Class pyjamas to bring me luck and snuggled into a borrowed sleeping bag by the side of the Maktesh Ramon Crater. I stared up at the velvet blackness of the night sky dotted with stars that I could not have imagined in a city. Out of the corner of my eye I saw a dark shape slinking up the slope in my direction like a desert fox. It was David moving his sleeping bag closer to mine.

The bathroom arrangements were as previously described. The lack of privacy brought its own internal problems. At night, I was guided to the women's wadi by a torch that Lars had lent me. Its heart wasn't in its task. The torch became weaker and weaker as the trip continued before it gave up altogether near Petra.

We rose early, eating breakfast round the campfire before sunrise. Our team of fair-haired, local guides with impeccable American accents had prepared a feast of tomatoes, cucumber, creamy white feta cheese and crusty bread. The coffee was piping hot, its welcoming aroma filling the air.

Our first visit of the day was to a desert animal reserve. David and I sat side by side on the bus. We found everything hugely amusing, filled with a special poignancy and meaning. We admired desert foxes with huge pointed ears that closed when there was a storm and learnt how particular breeds of donkeys and oryx were being reintroduced into the desert. I found these pioneering efforts to bring life to the desert moving.

We left Israel for Egypt at the border crossing of Eilat. David, hearing that we might go snorkelling in the Red Sea, bought us each a pair of goggles and snorkelling equipment. I liked his enthusiasm and generosity even if I wasn't sure I'd be trying out the equipment anytime soon.

"Can I see your passport photo?" I asked him while we waited in a queue that seemed to snake around the border town.

"It's not very good. I'm awfully old."

And there was the date of 19 November; it was not a chat-up line but the absolute truth. We had the same birthday. My mind began to whir, full of runic predictions.

The unexpectedly long wait to cross the border caused us to fall behind schedule. We stopped for the night on a sandy beach instead of heading directly to Mount Sinai.

This change of plan turned out well for David and me; the setting couldn't have been more romantic. The full moon was reflected in the gentle waves of the Red Sea, and the air was almost warm. It was altogether more welcoming than up the mountain.

"In Spain when I was growing up, we used to make three wishes on a full moon, one of which would come true," I told David, "but you mustn't tell anyone what you wish for, or it won't come true."

We had left behind our team of Israeli guides. The new Egyptian team accompanying us set up a cold, rice-based buffet on the wooden tables used by beach resort customers during the day. David unearthed a bottle of Chateau Laffite Laujac from his rucksack. We carried our feast to the water's edge. Snuggled side by side in our sleeping bags, our first kisses tasted of salt mixed with sand while we fought off an invasion of ants more interested in our supper than we were.

The next day, David climbed part of Mount Sinai on foot. I rode up on a camel. We stopped to drink Campari, the bottle kept cold in a clean, wet sock, with real slices of freshly cut orange. I was impressed by David's attention to detail; even on an arid mountain slope he produced the ingredients to add zest to our drinks. Refreshed we descended the mountain, my camel deciding to have a punch up with an ascending camel. Luckily they patched things up so we could continue our journey.

We spent the night on a secluded mountain ledge with just enough space for our sleeping bags. We could look down on the rest of the group. David, ever gallant, blew up my inflatable mattress. It made my nights softer, and I felt lucky he was there to take charge of the puffing.

One of the reasons for going on this study tour was to learn about the region and the historical events that had taken place in the time of Moses. Knowing how to strike the right rock in the right way to get a stream of water flowing out of it was a skill that could come in useful. Jim, a red headed, red bearded Texan in his

40s, instructed us daily. He was based at Jerusalem's Biblical Resources Study Centre. David and I nicknamed him His Eminence. It suited his flowing style. During his evening homily, David would fall asleep, his head in my lap, his snores not unnoticed by the group.

We admired the early Icons at St Catherine's Monastery before crossing into Jordan via Israel at the freshly reopened border. Many of us had collected stones and tiny pieces of flint. They were used as weapons by the Israelites fleeing Egypt.

Considering we were in the middle of the Intifada, the Palestinian uprising of the late 1980s and 1990s, we were lucky not to get into trouble at the customs. David was questioned about his computer, but the stones went undetected.

Campfire birthday

We celebrated our birthdays in Wadi Ramm; the desert valley made famous by Laurence of Arabia in the early 20th century. In the protective shadows cast by the surrounding rocks, we shared a birthday cake with candles, Jordanian wine and the bottles of champagne, our faces glowing from the campfire.

After dinner, David and I left the group for our evening stroll. These walks had become a ritual, allowing us to stretch our legs and admire the desert in the evening coolness, just the two of us. The five deserts have rock formations that differ in shape, colour and size. Each is unlike any other, unique in its stark beauty but at night, like cats, they all look alike. Yet, no matter how far we ventured from the camp, David was able to track our path through the rocks and get us back to the base. If it had been up to me, we would have got totally lost. I was too engrossed talking to him to notice which turning we had taken or register significant landmarks.

I prodded him about Doris. He told me how he had spent the past year getting to know her again, travelling to her home in Virginia and taking her to meet his children, family and friends in the US and Europe. He even got her a passport.

"What is it that you love about her?"

"I don't know. It was a second chance, the possibility to recapture what I had lost."

Perhaps they saw each other as they had been in their early 20s, he a handsome naval officer in uniform, she a blonde cheerleader. Out of the blue, after David's painful divorce and the fire that had burnt down Doris' home, the two had a chance to step back in time and relive their love. They had jumped at it before reality started to dawn. A Virginian country girl who brewed her own elderberry wine would have difficulty adapting to the lifestyle of a Geneva-based international lawyer and Burgundy wine buff.

Coincidentally there was a newly-wed couple in our party in their 70s. They had met up again when both were widowed, at a high school reunion. They had married so recently that the wife had not had time to change the name on her passport, causing a stir at one of the border crossings.

David and Doris had given it their best shot for more than a year. Now they were noticing differences that were too big to ignore. He told me how she had upset his son by smoking in his beloved car. Friends and family were putting the whole thing down to a mid-life crisis. I came along just at the right moment.

I have no photos of our birthday evening, only my memories and the black Bedouin outfit complete with veil that David had bought for me at an inflated price from our Bedouin guides. Earlier they had disguised us as a shy, nomad couple that had asked to be introduced to the group. At first everyone was taken in. The game was up when someone spotted my manicured fingers and our sensible Swiss hiking boots.

The fact that we agreed to be presented as a couple shows how our relationship was developing. I was very attracted to David. I found him handsome and sexy. He was generous and made me feel protected, taken care of, something I had rarely experienced in past relationships, possibly because I had not wanted to feel trapped.

Petra by moonlight

From Wadi Ramm, we journeyed north to the ancient city of Petra. Nyasi, our Bedouin guide, had grown up in these very caves before climbing giddy professional heights to become Minister of Tourism. He resigned when he was ordered to have his fellow Bedouins evicted from their caves. He knew the area like the back of his hand and treated us to an exceptional night-time tour through the winding passages of Little Petra. Flickering votive candles lit dark corners of the rock-carved cavernous temples while the reed like sounds of the traditional Jordanian Shababa could be heard in the background. We slept in a field nearby. David had found a spot below the last olive tree on the left that provided some privacy and shelter.

The next day we saw the ruins in daylight. Thanks to Nyasi's knowledge we were able to enter by little known back roads. Hand in hand, David and I visited the abandoned necropolis of temples and tombs cut into towering cliffs of red, pink and orange sandstone. Together we marvelled at the pediments and pillars that could have inspired William Kent had Petra been discovered in the 18th and not the 20th century. Afterwards, we rode on Arabian stallions to the only sauna located in a small tourist resort near the ruins.

It had been more than a week since my last bath. Although I kept my hands clean by rubbing them in the sand, I felt in need of a good scrub. Inside the discreet entrance, we were given towels and keys for the changing room. I went into the sauna while David had his massage. I didn't realize it was mixed until I got inside and found that I was sharing the heat with two men who looked as if they starred in a French Foreign Legion movie. One was large and wrapped in a towel and Arab headdress. He smoked a cigarette. The other was smaller and muscled. I didn't let my companions worry me. The heat seeped deep into my pores, cleansing me through and through.

After the heat came the massage. I lay down embarrassingly naked, clutching a flimsy towel while the masseur rubbed my skin vigorously. After each assault, he held up the black flannel for my inspection.

"Look Madame, black," he said. I had to agree.

"You had a male masseur?" asked one of my travel companions later, regretting that she had not taken up our offer to join us in the sauna.

Squeaky clean, we stepped outside and into the tourist boutiques that were a novelty after a shopping-free week. I bought us matching Jordan t-shirts with camels marching across our fronts.

"Now we look like a couple," said David, adding "a couple of what?"

Our fellow travellers did not need to see us in our matching t-shirts to realize that love was blooming in the desert. David and I had signed up for the trip because we were looking for the same thing. Yet we could have found peace and time to think on a quiet beach or up a mountain. Instead, we had chosen this trip because we both had a passion for the desert and its history. We were prepared to sleep in the open and face discomfort and even danger to experience it in the most natural way. Neither of us had expected to meet someone to share our passion, nor were we looking. And yet there we were, emerging from the wilderness, hand in hand.

Petra was our last stop in Jordan before crossing the border back into Israel. The journey took us through more magnificent landscapes to the Dead Sea. On its shores, Nyasi twisted an elegant turban from the black veil David had bought me. Then tied our wrists together with reeds that grew by the water. In Jordan, this meant that we would be married within the year.

Although I was not thinking of marriage, our relationship was advancing rapidly, faster than it would have had we been at home in Geneva. Like all holiday romances, we were swept up in a fairy tale that might or might not withstand the test of time.

Back to reality

Reality, when it hit, was brutal. In Tel Aviv while we were waiting to catch a plane home, we learnt about the massacre of 62 tourists in Luxor in neighbouring Egypt. It had taken place when we were in the Sinai and was a cruel reminder that violence erupted without warning in this holiest of places. We could have been amongst the dead, sudden victims of someone else's war.

David and I shared a taxi from the Airport to my Moillebeau flat. I offered him a drink and went into the bedroom to call my sister in London and let the family know that I was well. My mother was concerned about this trip when I'd first told her about it. She had thought that I was going as part of my work for the ICRC, not on holiday. She had been known to call me in Bosnia when I was there on mission.

My sister's news quickly removed all other thoughts from my mind. "Daddy is not well. It's bronchial pneumonia; it's very dangerous at his age," she told me.

"But he was fine when I last visited him in September. I told him all about the trip although I don't know how much he took in."

"He fell ill suddenly. His heart is strong, but his breathing was always his weak point. You'd better come quickly."

"I'll come at once. It's too late to get a flight now, but I'll be in Hove tomorrow."

David was in the living room looking out on the wooded garden. When I told him the news, he picked up his mobile phone and booked two tickets for Gatwick. It was a change to be with a man who could take care of everything; I had fended for myself for so long.

Hove in November was cold and bracing, the freshness

contrasting with the Red Sea air we had breathed the previous week. My sister and mother were at my father's bedside when we got to the nursing home. I was surprised to see my mother. My parents had divorced in the days when "Mental cruelty" was grounds for divorce. They had not seen each other for 15 years. And yet there she was to make her peace with her first husband, 18 years her senior.

"Tell your father you are getting married," she urged me. This suggestion was a far cry from her usual "Whatever you girls do, never get married" that had carried me through my adolescence. It was usually followed by "And don't have children." I did tell my father I was getting married although I was not thinking it; I had only known David a few weeks.

"I'm marrying David," I said. "We met in Jerusalem."

I'm convinced that he understood. Even though he was no longer conscious. I felt that he knew he could go in peace now that his eldest daughter would be taken care of, even without him.

For four days and nights we stayed in Hove. David and I were still together but in very different circumstances to the previous week. Every day we went to the nursing home to mount our vigil, searching my father's face for signs of improvement, an indication that the pneumonia was going away. The doctor couldn't give us much hope although he said that we could still be surprised.

My father died on Thanksgiving Day, a day of celebration for Americans. I wished David had been with me. He had returned to Geneva that day to spend Thanksgiving with his daughter, his ex-wife and her family. Daily life was gaining the upper hand over our desert romance.

Unlike his predecessors

Back in Geneva I was in turmoil. With my father's passing, a chapter of my life had closed. I began to realize how much I missed him, the subjects I would have loved to share with him. I felt insecure, homeless, like the victim of what the ICRC calls the forgotten conflicts.

At the same time, I was starting to realize that three weeks before my father died I had met my hero.

David was not like anyone I'd ever met. I had always gone for tall, skinny, dark-haired men, often with moustaches and glasses and a couple of years older than me. David did have the glasses! He was not very tall, slim but not skinny, with a generous smile and very blue eyes. He had grey hair and was exactly nine years and 20 minutes older than me.

The differences between David and his predecessors were not only physical. My boyfriends had been single with no intention of settling down. Some of them are interviewed in this book having married in their 40s, others are still single. David was the complete opposite. He had tried marriage three times which actually made him seem more mature and responsible. Although he had had three break-ups, he had also committed three times. If nothing else, he believed in the triumph of hope over experience.

David gave me the feeling that I could count on him; he wouldn't let me down. I felt I could trust him.

Hadn't I made a list of what I was looking for, you ask? Well, yes. After a long line of Mr Wrongs, I had discovered creative visualization. I had made a treasure map. It featured a series of ambitious, chic couples doing ambitious chic things like travelling to exotic locations, dancing till dawn against a background of golf courses and stately homes.

I had also listed my ideal partner's qualities. With hindsight, it described David rather well. I focussed on how I wanted him to be ready to make me the centre of his world. He should be well established, successful and established while we are at it. He should be sporty and sociable but not overly so and come from the New World.

In teeny-weeny letters, almost like an afterthought, I had written at the bottom of the page that I wanted him to be divorced, totally free of family ties. This was in deference to my mother's unhappy experiences with her two sets of in-laws.

Our first celebration

In December David and I went out to dinner to celebrate knowing each other for one month. We ended up at Le Francis. Once upon a time it had been glamorous. I had held my engagement party there many years before. It was not our first choice but in mid office party season and after numerous phone calls we were grateful to find a restaurant that could give us a table. When we arrived, we found out why. Le Francis had changed hands and gone from up-market to rather seedy Lebanese. We ordered mezze. Three tiny pieces arrived on a huge plate at an exorbitant price. We were undeterred. We thought it hilarious to be overcharged and underfed in gloomy surroundings. We were in love.

We spent Christmas with my family in London before taking our first trip alone together. We chose the Club Med in Senegal because I had heard it had a great golf course, wasn't too far to fly and was guaranteed sunshine. I had run a workshop in Dakar for the ICRC and had liked the people and the atmosphere.

The week would be a test. David and I would be together non-stop, just the two of us. I would come face to face with his compulsion to work even on holiday. David solved that one easily. He would get up early and do an hour's work. Then he'd climb back into bed, and we'd make love before breakfast. I can't say that our golf handicaps improved, but we did return to Geneva in fine form.

Our first argument

In February, we had our usual celebratory dinner on the 12th instead of the 13th because David had his daughter to stay on the 13th. We were starting to consider living together and planned to talk over a five-course dinner with vanilla in every dish.

The waiter had cleared away the mixed salad with vanilla pear vinaigrette and toasted walnuts when I asked David what he wanted in our future home. I prepared myself for my romantic partner to say something equally romantic such as a beautiful view, a bedroom with bay windows or an en suite bathroom with a Jacuzzi.

"I want a room for my daughter and I want to be within walking distance of my office."

The sole in a paper parcel with fennel, chives and vanilla lay untouched on my plate. The fish had died for nothing.

"You're not serious." I wailed, close to tears. "Are those the only things that matter to you? What about me, our living together, our relationship?"

The argument escalated around what mattered most to each of us. Before I knew what had happened, David stormed out of the restaurant to calm down. We didn't talk much on the drive to my flat where he dropped me off.

"What on earth is the matter?" asked a friend at work the next morning, seeing my red eyes.

"David and I go out for dinner every 13th of the month except yesterday we went out on the 12th because he has to keep his daughter on the 13th and..."

"Stop," she said. "You should never ever celebrate ahead of time. Forget it ever happened and go out together tomorrow, Valentine's Day." She was right.

The argument proved to me how much I cared about David. Arguments and even bust ups with other partners had always left me feeling slightly relieved in the midst of my unhappiness. This time there was no relief, only sadness and worry that we might not be able to sort it out.

I was still red-eyed when I saw David the next evening. We talked about misunderstandings and vowed to do better next time. It was a good lesson in how expectations can get us into trouble, how they need to be discussed and understood by both parties. I was expecting a romantic response from my partner, without saying as much. He was looking at the pragmatic. By talking it through calmly, we were able to concentrate on what we both wanted in order to protect what we had. It was dawning on both of us that our relationship really mattered.

The only losers in the story are the owners of a very nice little restaurant in Chambésy that will not be seeing us again for its vanilla-flavoured dinners.

The proposal at the Spa

The months went by, winter turning into spring. Like Bridget Jones and other singletons, I dreamt of mini-breaks with my beloved. David called me the "Mini-break Queen". He also enjoyed romantic weekends in glorious settings. We both love water; the sea in particular but a spa works too. One of our favourite spots was the Grand Hotel in Yverdon. Once installed on the fifth floor of the pale pink Belle Époque hotel, we'd soak in its outdoor heated pool with underwater jets. The only negative was that the weather was no better than in Geneva. Walking through the wet streets of the medieval city, huddling under shop awnings to shelter from the rain, it dawned on me that I wanted to marry David. I asked him in the doorway before we went in. He accepted. I had known since our big argument in February that this relationship was important to me; it took the arrival of spring for me to confirm my feelings.

Two hundred days to the wedding

I have never felt the need to have children, always felt that they might turn up "next year". Although my biological clock was ticking alarmingly, I had always been more concerned about not getting pregnant. Nevertheless, once we had decided to marry I made an appointment with a Californian gynaecologist at Geneva hospital who was specialized in pregnancies in the over 40s.

First I checked with David, "What do you think about having

a baby?"

"I'm honoured and flattered. I've never been asked before. Of course let's give it a try if you want to."

And so I did. I consulted the Californian gynaecologist, bought a thermometer and a book to record my temperature from day to day. Apart from writing in the book, I didn't give it much thought.

One hundred and eighty-four days to go

Our plan to move in together still held and I was busy house-hunting. Finding somewhere to live was a tall order in Geneva's tight housing market. To David's two requirements I had added my own of having a beautiful and spacious bedroom with en suite, easy access to a garden for my Yorkshire Terrier Drina and a study for each of us. We decided it would be fun to rent a house with its own garden. The beauty of Geneva is that it is possible to live in a house in the country within eight or ten minutes of the centre of town. It meant that we were not the only ones looking.

I called estate agent after estate agent. I was starting to despair when up came 22a avenue Pierre Odier. This was next door to my childhood home at 22-24 Pierre Odier. My stepfather had built the house in the late 50s. He sold it and built the two next door where I had been brought up with my sisters. Once again it seemed as if fate were taking a hand in our relationship by offering us this particular house, now a rental property.

The previous tenants, an American family of four, were moving back to Savannah.

"Y'all come anytime," said Brad who hailed from Georgia. "The door is not locked so you can visit but we won't be there between 12 and 2."

Oh to live so trustingly.

Naturally we liked it, more because of what it represented in my life than because it was a great house. We signed the lease; we would soon be in our own home.

One hundred and twenty-three days to go

July was busy. It was David's turn to propose which he did on bended knee in a Michelin starred restaurant in Thoiry, across the border in France. He has a sense of occasion and likes good restaurants, good food and good wine. Always has, always will.

We hadn't yet found a ring we liked. I pretended by transferring a beautiful emerald and diamond ring that he had given me for Christmas to my engagement finger.

One hundred and thirteen days to go

Later that month we moved into our new home, uniting our belongings and our lives from two different flats. We found ourselves with two complete bedrooms, most of the kitchen equipment in double and a phenomenal collection of books. The house was big enough for us to recreate David's room in one place and Lesley's room in another. It had three bedrooms on the ground floor and one in the attic as well as a huge downstairs with a room for David's cherry wood billiard table. His daughter could have her own suite, and we were on the right side of the Lake for David to get to his office with ease. My office was on the other side, but I was used to the crossing.

I had moved four times in the six years before I met David. I was used to hiring the movers to pack and unpack plates and glasses and put up pictures. I'd have everything in place within a week. Now I was part of a couple I was discovering the joys of having a man around the house to do all these tasks, but in his own time. I soon saw that the house needed a lot more work, and a husband-to-be couldn't be rushed to hang the pictures.

The house had two front doors.

"That way my father could come in and out without disturbing my brother and I," said my stepsister, who had lived there as a child.

"I want you to know that those bathrooms and the heating system are the originals," she added. She was right. The heating system broke down continuously, twice in one week the following February. David was good at fixing things, but heating systems were beyond even his "can do" approach.

Given that we already had more furniture than we knew what to do with, our first buys for our new home were for the garden. There was a two-seater swing with a canopy that made me feel slightly sick when it was in motion, then a dining table with an ancient Roman-look top covered in a vine leaf design and six chairs that could adapt to two positions. We added jolly striped green cushions. We were ready to invite.

Amongst our first guests was an old school friend who I had invited especially with her daughter of the same size as David's. I lit candles and made the Roman table look suitably festive. My friend's daughter thought it was great fun to pour the wax all over the table. Her mother's pleas for her to stop went unheeded. For the first time, David's daughter and I looked at each other with something like complicity as she offered to help clean up the melting mess. It didn't last.

"You have blue eyes. So do I," she told one of David's colleagues from his law firm, who was helping move a bed in through the first floor window.

"Blue eyes are the best." She looked pointedly at me. My eyes are dark brown.

Finding a way for the three of us to live in harmony was the biggest challenge that David and I faced together. Research shows that money and stepchildren are the two principle causes of marital breakdown: money is the cause for first marriage breakdown, children and stepchildren for subsequent marriages.

When I first visited David's flat his kitchen was papered with wall-to-wall photographs of his daughter. The doorbell sported his name and hers like husband and wife. At the time I wondered whether there was room for someone else in this couple, as did many of his friends.

I wanted to give being a family a try but with my lack of

experience I didn't know how to go about it and I didn't know the girl's mother well enough to discuss the matter. And so we stumbled on. Unused to children, I planned outings that never quite came off. We'd go for brunch at a hotel on the lake, and she'd crawl around under the table after piling her plate with chocolate. David tried visits to museums and aqua parks. None of it worked. My aunt made one of the better suggestions: the child could invite a school friend when she came to visit. We certainly had enough space in our house.

Ninety-two days to go

Installed in our new house, we wanted to have it blessed. We invited the Rector who had taken us to the desert, together with his wife, and some of our family and friends. We felt it to be a positive and good thing to do. In the sunny garden, life seemed to be smiling at us.

Seventy-four days to go

In early September, we flew to Washington DC where I was going to meet David's mother and sister. It was my first visit to the Nation's capital. I loved the Smithsonian, the architecture, the parks.

"Is there a President that you would like to see in particular?" asked the guide in charge of showing portraits of America's Presidents in the National Portrait Gallery.

"Yes. James A. Garfield," we replied in unison.

"In all my years here no one has ever asked to see James A. Garfield. I don't know much about him myself."

"He was born on 19 November, like us," we told her as we took in the bearded 19th century President who had had such a tragic destiny.

We drove from DC to David's mother's retirement community, about an hour's drive south in rural Virginia. The community was vast. It had houses for the fit as well as an assisted living facility where David's mother had been moved the previous month. There was a good restaurant, drug store, deli, shops, hairdresser, sports facilities and guest rooms. David's parents had originally bought a house there, but sadly his father died before they moved.

David had brought some black and white baby photos to break the ice between his mother and me.

"It's not because he was mine, but I've never seen a more beautiful baby," she said, holding up a photo of David in a sailor suit with his father and grandfather. Of course I agreed.

"You were a beautiful baby too," said my mother when I told her. She looked put out that someone else's first born could have been more beautiful than hers.

My future mother-in-law was a tall, thin and sociable lady. She painted New Mexican landscapes in powerful colours and beat all competition at Mahjong. She had met David's father at university where she was the only woman in their maths class.

She explained the numbering system for men in David's family. My David was D3; his father was D2 and his grandfather D1. His son who I had not yet met was D4. There had been a D0, but he wasn't talked about much.

I was pleased to be blessed with a wonderful mother-in-law. My regrets were that we lived an ocean apart and that I didn't have her around for long enough.

I was also pleased that the family was predisposed to like me. Years later Charlotte, David's brother's wife, told me how they had lived through the Doris saga.

When they heard about me, they said, "We don't care who she is, we like her."

In Virginia, we still had an important task to attend to; the purchase of our wedding rings, referred to as "tokens" based upon a play we had seen. David's blonde younger sister Anne, a serious shopper and a collector of Mall coupons, recommended a jeweller where we could find the ultimate token.

"I got a really good deal on a slightly coloured, cloudy

diamond, but I'm sure you'll like it," David told a shocked Anne and me in the car. It took us a few minutes before we realized he was teasing.

From Washington, we travelled to Long Island for the wedding of another late bloomer, Karen, who was marrying for the first time over 40, and Christian who was already a grand-father. A glamorous Long Island wedding, it featured white limousines, masses of bridesmaids and dancing till dawn in a traditional long house.

We must have enjoyed our stay in Montauk; I became pregnant.

Sixty-two days to go

After our wonderful birthday celebration around the campfire the previous November, we thought that the best follow up would be to marry on the same day the following year. The first person I phoned to share the good news was my mother. Her response took me aback.

"I can't possibly know where I'll be on 19th November. I could be in Sudan or Pakistan," she told me.

I asked her if she would like to buy my wedding dress thinking that this would make her feel more involved. She had flown to Paris to buy my dress for my third engagement party, some years before. This time she shirked the question.

It dawned on me that my mother's expectations had held me back from commitment when I was younger. No one was ever what she wanted as a son-in-law and now was no exception. But this time David and I were going ahead with our marriage. She did not come to our wedding nor did she acknowledge it, which was painful for both of us.

Fifty-eight days to go

I had imagined we would have our pick of reception halls in mid-November. How wrong I was. Our mutual birthday was also the sales week with the major auction houses commandeering Geneva's limited number of hotels. Never at a loss when it came to restaurants, David suggested romantic Chateau de Divonne in neighbouring France. We were in luck; they could give us a very pink private dining room as well as the bridal suite for the first night.

I turned my attention to what to wear for a November wedding. Ilona, who had predicted David's appearance all those months ago, recommended a young Swiss designer who had opened a shop in trendy Carouge. Together we decided on a double-sided coat and matching sheath dress in an unusual grey-green, silk on one side, matte on the other. I planned to wear my grandmother's brooch to close the coat at my neck.

I chose an ivory embroidered wedding dress with a high collar and cutaway shoulders, very Grace Kelly 1950s, for the reception. I added a wild silk shawl against the cold and off-white heels. I had chosen them in the basement of a London shoe shop. It housed wall-to-wall wedding shoes and twenty-something's also hunting for the elusive shoe. We bonded as we discussed the merits of each style.

Thirty days to go

There were administrative details to settle too. One month before the wedding, David and I went to the Chêne-Bougeries Registry Office to sign a promissory letter declaring our intention to marry.

I couldn't get out of the car.

"Would you like to walk around the grounds before we go in?" asked David, seeing me panic.

"Yes I would."

It took me 20 minutes of walking round the communal gardens outside the Town Hall before I had the courage to go in. It wasn't that I didn't want to marry David. It was my fear of committing to anyone. I had reached the age of 45 without getting married, in spite of three engagements, and I was frightened of committing to the wrong person. For me marriage meant for life, divorce didn't enter into it after what I'd seen of my parent's experience.

When we pushed past the wooden door of the Mayor's office, I took a deep breath and signed. David had already signed without blinking an eye. I felt better once I had followed suit. I was ready to meet the Lady Mayor who was going to marry us. She owned a chemist and was kindness itself, suggesting cold remedies for the pregnant lady that I was then.

Twenty days to go

That month, I went to Stockholm to attend an ICRC donors meeting. My first glimpse of the Swedish capital was under early snowflakes.

Ilona was waiting for me at Geneva airport. She had arranged a surprise hen party at her flat. I was very touched, and though we have lost touch I hope that my speech at her 40th showed how I had valued her friendship.

Fourteen days to go

Then everything started to go wrong. My fairy godmother who had given me a shove in David's direction from the start suddenly let me down, leaving me alone to deal with two terrible events.

First, our house was burgled. It happened in the afternoon when we were both at work. Suddenly Drina's little furry body and pointy ears flashed through my mind. I needed to give her a hug when I got home. She was alone in the house with the thieves. Maybe she had been communicating telepathically with me. The burglars took my grandmother's brooch that I had worn to sign the promissory letter. I had taken if off the next day because I was going swimming and didn't want to leave it in the changing rooms. I didn't think that, in safe Geneva, we risked daylight robbery.

The loss of my grandmother's jewellery was heart breaking. My father had given it to me, and it was as if I had lost him for a second time. I had planned to wear the brooch on my wedding day, at my neck. Soon to be sister-in-law, Anne came to the rescue. She gave me a coral cameo that had belonged to her, and David's, grandmother.

The burglars made a thorough search of the ground floor, taking our still unworn wedding tokens from their hiding place in the back of the desk drawer. Here, at least, was a silver lining. I had chosen a ring with three colours of gold as David's wedding band. With hindsight, it was hideous. Thanks to the burglars I was able to choose a simple gold band that suited him much better, paid for by the insurance. My father would have paid for my wedding had he been alive. In the end, I used the insurance money from the jewellery he had given me. I also bought myself an art deco bracelet of gold that had my mother-in-law's initials and birthday engraved on it. I was touched by the coincidence.

Seven days to go

The second tragedy was another robbery. I miscarried following the burglary. I was unsettled and left alone in a house that had just been burgled. David was accompanying his daughter to her riding lessons. Hormonally challenged, my state of mind was delicate. I dreamt that I would give birth to my dog Drina. That was fine with me, but within nine months my dream Drina would turn into a child acting similar to David's daughter. She could drive a wedge between us.

On our next visit to the gynaecologist I learned that there was no longer a heartbeat, no longer a new life. He booked me into the clinic, a week before our wedding. David stayed with me all day. It was the first time that the reality of being a woman and able to give life, touched me. I didn't try to get pregnant again. I wonder if I took the right decision.

I kept the photo of the embryo. "Spot" we called it because of its beginnings as a blue spot on a pregnancy test, and something more; in our wedding photos a circle is clearly visible over our heads.

"Who is the little girl that should have been at your wedding?" asked a psychic friend. I am sure it was the daughter we never had.

In the one year and six days leading to my marriage, I had lost my father, my jewellery and now my baby. My immediate family was not by my side. It was difficult to understand why such painful events occurred in what should have been the happiest year of my life.

I regret that marriage preparation was not available in Geneva at the time. David had been much married; I was over 40 and had never been married. We had to adapt to each other and deal with past baggage. I would have loved to talk it over with a competent facilitator. One thing we did do was to write the hymns and the service for the blessing of our marriage ourselves. It took place six months after the registry office ceremony. Jelte, a friend and Pastor who married us, told me that by so doing we had taken the rare opportunity to talk through what we wanted for our lives together. She felt this to be an important step in our understanding of each other.

One day to go

Our house was filling up for the wedding. To our delight David's son D4 flew in from Seattle, changing flights at least four times to be with us.

"You don't think I'd let you get married without me?" he asked his father. At D4's wedding in 2012 we were three Mrs D3s, but that's another story.

A Scottish lawyer friend from London, bearing snail plates and forks as a wedding gift, was staying with us, as was Bex, the best man, passing through from Virginia with his wife, son and son's wife.

"You are very brave to have a house full of strangers before your wedding," said Bex's wife, Judy.

I didn't mind; in keeping with tradition I was staying with Joanna, my best woman in her flat overlooking the lake.

Joanna had planned a second hen party for me with Ilona and Judy. We represented four different facets of womanhood. Judy, the oldest had been married in her 20s. Mother of three, she had recently returned to work in logistics, a lifesaver for her. Next came Bernese Joanna who had never married but had a long-term partner. She had been private secretary to a member of the British aristocracy in Paris until his death and now spent her time lowering her golf handicap and looking after her four properties. She liked the persistent way I set about learning golf. I liked her free spirit. Then there was me, about to be married for the first time. Ilona, my ICRC colleague, was the youngest. She was single and met her partner some years later in her 40s. She gave me a garter as "my something new."

The big day

Joanna had promised David to get me to the Town Hall on time. We had arranged for the photographer, Mauricio, brother of a graphic designer I had worked with, to take photos of us from her home. I put on thigh highs with a lacy top; the garter Ilona had given me and my green dress and coat.

When it came to my makeup, I had had a trial with an artist, but she had made me look like my mother.

"Sooner or later we all look like our mothers," she told me.

I did my own makeup for the most important day of my life.

Back at the house all was chaos. David had got his guests to the Town Hall only to discover that the jet-lagged best man had forgotten the rings. This at least kept his mind off whether his bride would turn up at the Registry Office or not. He was convinced that I wouldn't, based on my history of bolting but had his camera at the ready just in case. He snapped me through the window as we were arriving.

At ten minutes to three, there I was, relaxed and smiling. I walked into the Registry Office on David's arm, both of us grinning from ear to ear.

"The bride usually looks happy at her wedding. It is rare to see a groom look as happy as David does," remarked Joanna.

All my friends were there, in spite of it being a Thursday afternoon. This made me smile even more. The Lady Mayor looked splendid in her robes and chain. She talked about how fate had brought David, born in Annapolis, Maryland and Lesley, born in London, to marry in the Chêne-Bougeries Town Hall.

We said "Oui" and slipped the rings on each other's fingers. We were man and wife about to spend the rest of our lives together. I felt dizzy and filled with happiness, smiling even more than before. This was a whole new experience. David and I were now joined in the eyes of the law. We had decided that, in six months, we would do it again, in the eyes of God when we intended to write the ceremony and hymns ourselves.

Together we signed the registry with our witnesses and stepped out into the golden autumn sunshine to have our photos taken in the immaculate gardens. We posed under a big oak tree. Meeting my stepson D4 for the first time, I hugged him. The photos show how relaxed and happy we all looked. Even Drina had a partner, Nico, a giant French sheepdog.

We returned home to the house built by my stepfather to tuck into Turkish mezzes and sip champagne. Later, light headed, we bundled our houseguests into cars and set off for the Chateau de Divonne, some 45 minutes' drive away. The Americans pulled out their passports, loving the idea of going to another country for dinner.

We were spending our first night as husband and wife in the bridal suite on the first floor of the Chateau. It was decorated with huge red chintz tea roses on the walls, the curtains, the bedspread. Joanna zipped me into my dress. It bagged a little at the top where I had lost weight. Drina was excited, jumping up at the stiff, hooped petticoat to reach me. Joanna looked spectacular in black with golden appliqued flowers across her front.

On the gallery, I paused and looked down. David was waiting for me at the foot of the stairs, showing off his legs and his Scottish origins in a kilt. He ran upstairs to take my hand and lead me down the sweeping staircase, the billowing skirt of my wedding dress standing up by itself and buoying me along. I felt complete; I had signed on the dotted line, and I knew it was the right thing to do.

We sipped champagne before going into the dining room to seat our friends at four tables. Our witnesses and their families, D4 and Karen and Christian were at the top table with us. Dinner was delicious. The Chateau de Divonne was known for its cuisine, and we had paid several visits to sample the different dishes. After dinner came the speeches. My groom spoke lovingly, using his oratory skills as a lawyer to reconfirm his place in my heart. Joanna talked of my wish to have a family around me and had me, and many of the guests, in tears, while Bex gave a clever speech involving letters and numbers.

To celebrate we had chosen birthday cake instead of wedding cake. Two round lemon cakes were wheeled in complete with candles, shooting sparklers and birthday wishes.

We had also planned a competition. Everyone was given copies of a photo of us on camels so that they could fill in the speech bubbles of either the camel or the human couple. The winners had chosen the camels; one camel saying, "What a guy he must be smitten, he can't stop laughing and smiling" and the other camel replying "I wish you'd talk to me like that."

Then it was time to go upstairs and spend our first night together as Mr and Mrs David A. Lawson III, my first night as a married woman.

The next day we sobered up and took our out of town guests for lunch at La Librairie, a restaurant in central Geneva before leaving for the airport.

Postscript to the wedding

I don't think I realized that I was married until our honeymoon in Mauritius. We were on the beach, soaking up the sunshine when an insistent voice behind me called,

"Mrs Lawson, Mrs Lawson." I looked around for my mother-in-law before realizing that the waiter was speaking to me.

The significance of what I had done dawned some weeks later. Over lunch in Geneva with friends I looked across the table at David. As he gestured, I caught sight of the ring that I had put on his finger two weeks before and which he never takes off. In a flash it occurred to me that I had made a commitment to him, I had told the world that this is the man I love. I was no longer standing on the outside looking in; I was married, one of a partnership.

I had set off on a quest of discovery that had culminated in 200 days leading to my wedding. It had been full of joy and pain. A new chapter of my life was beginning. In order to get there, I had had to make tremendous changes in my expectations. In some ways, my meeting and falling in love with David was like a fairy tale, but the reality was more prosaic. I had set off on an Odyssey to meet my true love and in the process had had to overcome painful hurdles.

When a friend said, "You were just lucky to meet David," I have to wonder what she was on about.

Perhaps it was luck to choose that particular trip, although it would not have been everyone's first choice. Perhaps it was luck that we had the same birthdays. Perhaps it was more luck that neither of our current partners was able to join us. But the events we shared and came through together, the decisions we took and the way we adapted to each other in order to spend our lives as one, took love, not luck. Today we can look back on that first year as building the foundations of our marriage, a construction that we continue to add to every day.

Part II

Five Steps to Marriage over 40

Step One:
The Call

This is the beginning of your journey. You picked up this book because you are not totally happy with your private life. Something or rather someone is missing: a partner to share your life. You feel like the odd one out in the world of smiley couples. Perhaps your mother or your colleagues nag you about your single status. To top it off your 40th birthday is looming or has been and gone.

You have heard The Call. It is time for change.

Step One will help you to:

- *Take responsibility in your relationships*
- *Review your expectations*
- *Identify your must-haves*
- *Recognise relationship patterns*
- *Rethink your space, relook your home*
- *Draw your treasure map*

By setting the scene in this way you will prepare a path to a new type of relationship.

One thing has to be clear as the day from the outset; you have the right to a loving, supportive relationship. Ah, but there's a hitch, you say. You want to love and be loved and yet finding and keeping a committed relationship has presented a continuous challenge up until now. Either you meet someone who likes you but you don't fancy them or vice versa. The big Four O has come and gone and you are still no nearer to finding the person who will share your life. Don't despair; with this book in your hands, you are ready to achieve your relationship objectives. Like in a fairy tale, you have answered The Call.

This first Step finds you at home. Perhaps you have a job you like, friends and a great place to live. Your life is basically satisfactory, yet something is missing. It becomes more obvious at holiday times when you start looking for someone to go away with, or on Sunday mornings when you'd like to have someone to cuddle or when you notice that your single status excludes you from invitations to dinner parties. You are fed up with buying meals for one or being sat at the table behind the pillar after being asked "Table just for one". In a nutshell, you are missing a partner to share your life.

This is making you feel if not wretched at least not fully satisfied with the situation.

In Step One, you are going to take a calm look at what could be holding you back and preventing you from having that special relationship. After all you are bright and smart and talented and loveable, there has to be some obstacle that is blocking your path to true happiness. Once you have identified what it might be, you will learn to understand and deal with it more effectively. Then you can focus on what you really want and how to get it.

You are not alone in your quest. Others have overcome their demons, men and women who faced challenges, just like you. Some of their stories will ring bells. They are interspersed with exercises that will further assist you to leave the old ways behind.

Take responsibility in your relationships

"To say you have no choice is to relieve yourself of responsibility."
Patrick Ness, *Monsters of Men*

You are going to begin by jumping straight into the deep end. If relationships haven't worked in the past, it could be because you are not exercising your right to choose. You do have a choice; it's up to you to take it. How much responsibility do you take usually when it comes to choosing a partner? Before applying for a job, at the very least you research the company, look at your network to see if you know anyone who works there and discuss it with your contacts. You go through the interview process and if all goes well you are offered the job. You then have to decide if it's what you really are looking for, whether it advances your career. You will weigh up the pros and cons and finally decide whether to take it or not. It is rarely a snap decision unless you have to find something quick to pay the rent. The same rules should apply when you are looking for a partner.

You want the best relationship possible, and of course you deserve the best, You need to be sure that you are taking responsibility for it, not waiting on the side-lines for life to come knocking at your door. It might, but you have to give it some encouragement.

If your relationships always seem to go in the wrong direction, it might be because you are letting yourself be chosen not choosing. You are not going to be happy with the result because it is not your decision. Here is a clue:

Do you carry on doing what you've always done when you meet someone new, even when experience has shown you that it doesn't work?

If you answered yes, well done for admitting it. Being a victim doesn't just happen. It is up to you. You can choose to let life and others control what happens to you or you can step up and take the commands yourself. This first exercise will show you how.

Exercise 1

Look at the statements below. They have in common the fact that they are putting the blame on someone else. Have you heard yourself saying one or other of them? By doing this, you are giving your power to another person and taking away your own sense of responsibility. It's a dangerous game. While it's easy to blame someone else and not take responsibility for your actions, don't be surprised if the end result is not the one that you wanted.

1. You make me really angry.
2. Why do bad things keep happening to me?
3. It's not my fault, if you'd had a childhood like mine you'd know.
4. I've given up on relationships, they never work out.
5. Look what you made me do.
6. No way am I going to trust others, they always let me down.
7. All I wanted was a good relationship with you.

Look at those statements again. How could you rephrase them to assume responsibility yourself? For example, you could turn "You make me really angry" into "I get angry." It puts you into the control seat doesn't it?

Now rephrase any of the statements that are relevant to your situation in a manner that gives you the responsibility for the action and the outcome.

It isn't easy but the more you practice, the more naturally change and empowerment will come to you.

Willow's story

By the time Willow was in her early 40s she had had eight boyfriends. Each had lasted one year or more. She knew that the relationships were not worth pursuing and so did her family and friends, in particular her father. He pointed out the immaturity of her partners. In spite of the warnings, she would stick it out with each one for at least 12 agonizing months. She sees her passive stance as the root of the problem:

I was chosen instead of choosing. These men were more interested in me than I was in them. I was not emotionally mature enough to see them as they really were. Once we were involved it became me trying to please them, I had to make it work. With hindsight, I realize that my self-esteem was not as high as it should have been.

Willow considers that both your heart and your head have to be involved in your decision. Only then will you have the maturity to be able to choose the best person to meet your needs:

My heart was not mature enough. I needed to go through several experiences before I recognised the right partner for me. I saw men like items on the menu. I was looking for character traits instead of the person that would suit me. It was not till my late 30s that my heart started to catch up with my head. Of course, you need to be intellectually discerning but your heart has to be there too. You have to feel that it's right. For some people, it can be the heart that is ready, but not the head. They want to have fun, enjoy themselves, but not accept reality. In either case, when it's the best choice you don't have to spend time convincing yourself.

In one of the most important decisions in her life, Willow had played the passive role. Of course it is flattering to be chosen by someone, initially. If you have ever looked for a puppy and felt a soft furry paw tapping your ankle when you thought that you were the one doing the choosing, you'll know what I mean. But it can lead to the wrong decision. Even more so with a partner. Both halves of the couple need to feel responsible or one of you is bound to be dissatisfied.

Staying in a relationship too long as Willow did, either because you are hoping that it will change or because you are frightened of being alone, is not a solution. Many of the couples in this book regretted staying too long with the wrong person. Don't let that be your case. There are other options out there.

Review your expectations

"A wonderful gift may not be wrapped as you expect."
Jonathan Lockwood Huie

I once read an article in an English paper that asked, "What is a nice girl like you doing still single?"

The unmarried journalist who wrote the piece replied tongue in cheek that in her experience, the nice girls are single, it is the scheming, manipulative ones that are in couples. They are the ones who know what they are looking for and have the confidence to go out and get it. Without being that categorical, there is value in knowing what you want, in having expectations. Like Sylvie who decided to commit because she had had enough of repeating the pattern of painful relationships that went nowhere. She was 25 when she married so her story is not included in this book.

Nevertheless it is illuminating to see her pragmatic view of marriage; suffering was not for her. You will learn more about this in Step III. For the moment be aware that when you have to ask too many "Should I, shouldn't I" questions in the early stages of your relationship, you are working too hard.

Expectations are also the behaviours you expect from other people. You have expectations of everyone in your life, including the people you work with, your best friend and your family. You expect your salary to be in the bank on payday. You expect to hear from your parents on your birthday. You expect the person you're dating to call, or text, within a certain timeframe after a date. These are all perfectly reasonable expectations. It's only when you set them too high, and your standards are not met that you wind up feeling sad or angry.

Perhaps you were brought up to expect that there is one perfect person for you. From childhood your dreams were peopled with handsome princes or beautiful princesses who would one day sweep you off your feet. You were talked into believing that there was someone special just for you; your *media naranja* (half orange from the Spanish proverb). No one else would do. As a result you set the bar very high for your new partner. The slightest indication that they did not meet your standards such as wearing unfashionable shoes or appearing awkward around your friends and that person was out. You might have overlooked their other qualities and ignored real red flags in the process. Throughout this book you will learn that within a certain framework, there are many people who would suit you very well, as long as they respond to your heart's desire. The recently popular idea of there being only one perfect person for you is a myth, there are many candidates out there who could make you happy.

Exercise 2

To set the bar of your expectations at the right height, you need to determine what will make you happy. Do you know the qualities, values, characteristics and lifestyle that you want to find in your future partner? I see in my practice that it can be difficult for singles to identify what they want, however nearly all can come up with a convincing description of what they don't want.

With this in mind begin by thinking about your most recent or significant relationship. What didn't you like about it? Think back and ask yourself the following questions, being really, really honest.

1. What did you totally dislike about that person?
2. What were your feelings when the relationship failed?
3. Was it your fault, your partner's fault or circumstances? Be specific.
4. What irritated you in the relationship?
5. What do you absolutely not want to show up again in future relationships?

Take your time to answer these questions. What are your answers telling you? Perhaps you gave answers to questions 1 and 4 on the lines of "I always had to pay" or "We didn't have sex often enough" or "My partner didn't get in touch often enough." This will help you answer question 5.

When you have finished you have two options; either throw away your answers to get rid of the negativity or keep them to remind you of what you don't want, ever, ever, again.

Susanne's story

It is essential to know what you are looking for in a partner, but not to typecast and insist that only a particular style of person could be your match. Swiss academic Susanne was convinced that only someone with a similar education to her own could make her happy. She had been to good Swiss and English universities and would only consider a future partner from a similar background; a manual worker was quite out of the question. She wanted a man of her age, in his early 40s, who, like her, had never been married before. She decided to try the Internet but got very little response to her online profile because her criteria were so rigid:

> In the past I tended to fall for the "wrong" men, when picking them myself. Whenever one of very few relationships I had was supposed to become more serious, the men tended to leave. Only with the last one was I the one to leave because he wanted to talk me out of my wish for children.
>
> That negative experience made me realize what I was doing wrong. I decided to make a special effort, out of defiance, to intensify my search for a partner. In the process I discovered my future husband's profile and contacted him.
>
> I don't believe in "the one" any longer, rather I think that there are hundreds of men out there with whom you could make a loving relationship work. It is more a case of you choosing by your own decision and will to make him "the only one" for yourself, even more so by marrying him. It is a serious commitment, a great responsibility and a wonderful opportunity for personal growth and another dimension of depth to love.

Susanne's expectations concentrated on exterior traits – good education, academic profession, same age, never married. It was only when she looked at his inner qualities instead of his outward appearance that she found her man. Her change of approach brought Paul into her life quite quickly:

In his profile he had quoted, "The most beautiful thing on earth is to love and be loved." This sentence could have been written by me. I decided to contact him on the spur of the moment, although I had had some reservations about his technical profession. I had this idea that someone with a similar academic education would suit me best. The online dating test revealed that we had much in common with regard to personality, interest and habits, and this truly shows in a positive way.

His profile prompted her to act out of character and respond to him quickly. How they met up and what happened next is in Steps Three and Four.

Oliver's story

At the other end of the spectrum, low self-esteem can lead you to set the bar too low with equally disastrous results. If a friend tells you after a break-up, "It could have been worse, you could still be with him," you might need to raise your expectations.

Oliver, the central character in the film *Beginners* is a good example of this scenario. He is a single man nearing 40 with a history of failed relationships. He discusses his latest debacle with his father's dog, something of a philosopher on four paws. Oliver can't understand what went wrong when his new girlfriend moved in, why he didn't feel right with her and why he let her move out without following her. The dog lets Oliver know through subtitles that he, Oliver, anticipates that the relationship will fail before it even begins.

Like Oliver, perhaps you think that you would love to have someone to share your life, yet when it comes down to it you are frightened of taking that huge step. In the meantime, you content yourself with making the wrong choices and accepting second best. By choosing the wrong person, time and time again, you protect yourself from committing. After all, you can't really be expected to settle down with someone totally unsuitable. If you feel an unexpected sense of relief after a break up or even just after an argument, it could be your gut feeling telling you that this is the wrong person.

Identify your must-haves

As you have seen, being too rigid or too lax in your expectations can lead you into trouble. In exercise 2, you looked at what you don't want. Now let's look at what you do want. Most of the women and a few of the men in my survey made a list of what they were looking for. Interestingly, their lists did not always correspond to the partner they eventually met.

Shane Watson, in her book, *How to meet a man after 40, and other midlife dilemmas solved*, talks about how she was set up with her future husband three years before their official meeting. She discarded him with a "You cannot be serious rating" based on the list that she had made. In her book she gives some of them. They included the fact that he was very recently divorced, he had three children in tow, a savage haircut and that he was wearing a brown shirt. Even more important for her was "his suburban postcode, an indication that he was living an awkward divorcee's life, complete with barbecues in the back garden of his second time round house."

He was so clearly not what she was looking for in her opinion that she lost track of him until chance brought them back together three years later. This time they clicked. The lesson to be learnt is to give someone a fair chance in spite of their haircut or their shirt. You never know.

Lori Gottlieb showed how expectations can lead singles to overlook interesting opportunities. She tried an unusual experiment in her book *Marry Him, the Case for Settling for Mr Good Enough*. First she interviewed a group of single women. Then she interviewed their ex-boyfriends who had all since married. Finally, she spoke to the wives of those ex-boyfriends turned husbands.

She discovered that the single women had found a deal

breaker in their former partners of a very superficial kind. One hadn't seen a favourite film, one was too predictable, yet another was loosing his hair. The wives were similar in every way to the single women except for one distinguishing feature: the ability to redefine romance in terms of what they had, not their wish list. For example, the wife of the man who was losing his hair recognized that by 45, most men are losing their hair.

Exercise 3

Now that you know what you don't want and have fixed your expectations at a realistic level, it's time to think of the qualities that you really want your partner to have. Imagine that you are looking for a new home. You would write down whether you want a house or a flat, the number of bedrooms and bathrooms you require, the neighbourhood and the price you are prepared to pay. These are the basics, but they might not bring you your perfect home. For that, you need to add the senses.

It's the same for a partner. Consider your requirements; the qualities that make the relationship work for you. This is not the tall, dark and handsome stuff. Remember that your past partners might all have been respectively tall, dark and handsome or blonde and bubbly and yet you are still alone. The exercise on what you don't want will have given you some pointers.

These are the inner qualities that will put a spring in your step as you think of them on your way to work. They might include:

- Must be kind
- Makes you the centre of their world
- Makes you laugh
- Gets on with your dog/children/mother

The important thing is to list what matters to you inside the person, not just the outward appearance and attributes.

Once you have your list, and it should include at least 10 features, you need to identify the most important. Those are the five that you really can't live without. Write them on post-its and move them around the table to help you decide which one comes top of the list.

Think about each carefully. To go back to the house example, what do you really need to make a house a home? Perhaps a house without a garden wouldn't work for you.

Imagine your dream garden, the type and colour of flowers

growing there, whether there is grass or paving stones, the smells, the textures. Whether you would have chairs and a round table, a hammock, swings. Do the same for the five essential qualities that you want in your partner. If you have listed "makes me laugh", think about what makes you laugh, the situations, jokes, books and plays that tickle your sense of humour.

Be specific. In the flat analogy, you had to remember to account for all the rooms, otherwise you could end up with a great flat with a tiny kitchen. And you love cooking. It's the same here. If you like playing tennis and golf, you need to work on what those sports bring to mind. A golfer is probably resistant, out in all weathers and for long periods of time. A tennis player has shorter, sharper bursts of energy. Don't just say, "Likes sports" as you might find yourself with a footballer instead when you hate team sports.

Carry on through your list until you can really see, feel, smell and hear your five essentials. Focus fully on them, and learn what works for you. Soon those five essential characteristics will start showing up around you. In the house analogy, if you really want a house with a fireplace you will notice how often houses with fireplaces come on the market. With a partner, by focussing on what you want, you are bringing your dreams closer to reality.

Nathalie's story

Author and dancer Nathalie married in her early 40s, having all but given up on finding love:

For years, I had tried all sorts of things. I read Tarot cards, I visualized the ideal man and relationship, I wrote affirmations, I joined clubs, I took flower essences, I wrote long lists and burned them as offerings, and I put the word out. My requirements became progressively simpler: Be able to fell a tree and be able to lift me. I got that person, but it turned out he thought phoning every other week and making no plans whatsoever was his ideal relationship; he was more involved with his sister than with me!

I had two long-term relationships, each lasting 5 years or more, before I met my partner. The most recent relationship had ended and started again and ended and started yet again in a cycle of frustration and disappointment. In the last relationship, there was a pattern of chase and capture and then a lack of commitment to intimacy. Perhaps the lack of commitment was an inability for intimacy in disguise between the two of us. I wasted a lot of time on that relationship and it still makes me sad.

By the time I met my husband, my requirement was incredibly simple: I wanted someone kind. Honestly, that was it. I just wanted a man who was kind. To me, that implied that he would be caring and he would listen and he would communicate. My husband does not know how to fell a tree and he has a wonky back so he never lifts me!

I think life can be incredibly exacting, and the most important quality, what lasts, is kindness. By the time I was 37, I have to say that I'd given up on ever having a stable relationship. Really, I thought forget it. I even told my husband when we first met that I was planning on having "a series of hounds, of dogs, of creatures full of fur and love." I had completely and totally given up on men. I wasn't angry; I didn't have expectations; I was just completely detached and focused on having doggies. I think that this detachment prepared me to meet someone. I had stopped worrying.

Recognize relationship patterns

"Unless commitment is made, there are only promises and hopes... but no plans."
Peter F. Drucker

Being clear about your wants and needs can also help you recognize if there is a behaviour that keeps preventing you from committing to a stable relationship. Then you can work on it. When you know why, for example, you keep ending up with a version of the same person time and time again, why you never let yourself get too close or what you are frightened of, you will have the tools to break the cycle.

Your past relationships can once again give you clues about what is going on. They are wise teachers.

Exercise 4

Write down the names of your most significant past partners in a column. Next to each, list their different traits, both positive and negative. Part of your ex's attraction might have been how their negative behaviours fitted in with your own. If you are always late, a partner who is also late might attract you initially but irritate you further down the line. Likewise if you are ambiguous about committing, you could be attracting others who are also ambiguous, even when you are not aware that you are. They could be recognising a kindred spirit in you.

Look at your list of ex partners.

1. Do you have a pattern of choosing a person with particular characteristics, only to end up unhappy with your choice? Perhaps you are attracted to out-going, sociable people when actually you like to stay at home by the fire.

2. Are there some negative traits that always seem to show up in a partner and eventually drive you berserk? You found their forgetfulness quite touching in the beginning but after a while it got on your nerves.

3. What about the positive qualities? Are they in your big five? There is no use meeting someone who loves gardening and flowers when you have hay fever, metaphorically speaking.

4. Do your relationships seem to break up for the same reasons every time? Answers to the three previous questions will help you here.

When you've answered the questions, notice if there is a pattern. Can you give it a name? How would you do things differently knowing this?

Frank's story

Frank's fear of commitment had him attracting women who were not right for him, over and over:

Friday plus Saturday was long term for me before I met my wife. I broke off two engagements. I think I was too young, I didn't know what I wanted but it certainly wasn't marriage. To me, it seemed like a prison sentence, a loss of freedom. On top of it, I wouldn't have wanted to be in the type of marriages I saw around me. I was immature and besides I liked to enjoy myself.

Although I was looking for fun, I kept finding myself with women who wanted to spend more time with me than I wanted to spend with them. There was always conflict.

Why did Frank think he attracted needy women?

I was more interested in what they looked like than what was inside. The more attractive the woman, the more insecure she was.

By the time I was 40, I had realized if I didn't do something different I would be 50 with a ponytail, driving a Corvette Stingray and chasing young girls. I had to change everything in my dating pattern.

As a first step, I decided to attend a three-day personal development seminar. It was about self-discovery and that's what it delivered. I learnt that my emotional availability was limited; I was reserved, protected, not vulnerable enough. I had to be more open to having relationships with my friends as well as with a potential partner. I needed to be less selfish, more present in relationships.

The first seminar was just the start. I took some follow up seminars. The whole thing was a good learning experience. I had left home at 15 and learned what I learned on the road. Now I had to practice doing something different every day to bring new energy into my life.

I did make a list of qualities that I was looking for in a woman. My first list was very superficial, mentioning things like attractive and athletic. When it came to revising my list, I realized I wanted someone I could really get on with, who had her own life, not needy like my past girlfriends. There had to be a degree of trust and we both had to have different aspirations.

Frank pursued his interest in personal development, little knowing that this change in his attitude would bring about change in his personal life:

I was attending a seminar on wealth consciousness. In the end, the group went on a 10-day trip but we didn't know where until we got to the airport. We went to Thailand. My future partner was running the company in Arizona and I was living in Las Vegas at the time. At the airport, she was looking around to see who she wanted to hang out with on the trip. I introduced myself. We had a handshake deal that whatever happened in Thailand stayed in Thailand. When we got back in January, we stayed in touch. I flew to Arizona on 14 February and we went on a date but we'd agreed it was not a Valentine's Day date.

Then we started seeing each other. I was flying up to Arizona, buying flowers, gifts, and surprises. On her birthday she went to a restaurant with 12 women friends, I surprised her by showing up and buying dinner for everyone. After that, she started to come to Vegas. We dated at a distance from January to August. I left my job and moved to Arizona in August and in March of the following year we married. I moved for love.

Frank's partner is unlike his past girlfriends physically and emotionally:

She is a red head, not blonde. She's also smart and assertive and laughs at my jokes. She doesn't take things seriously. My previous girlfriends were so insecure if I said anything that could be construed as negative. She just laughs. She doesn't care about my attitude.

Frank's transformation began with an awareness which lead him to take personal development seriously. Once he had made that shift towards commitment and connection with others, he was able to recognise and welcome a new partner into his life. He was able to enter into a relationship that broke the mold of his past experiences, one that enabled him to build a new life.

I got my Masters in Business Administration at 38, late. Then I married and had a kid in my 40s. I did everything late in life. I had to experiment a lot just to grow up, possibly because I was so affected by the divorce of my parents.

Beverley's story

"After all, it's one thing to run away when someone's chasing you. It's entirely another to be running all alone."
Jennifer E. Smith, *The Statistical Probability of Love at First Sight*

Moving on before you become attached can be your way of avoiding commitment. When your work requires you to move frequently from place to place, it can complicate your quest to meet potential partners. Hard workers who put their all in to defend their career are praiseworthy. It could be time to take stock if you find yourself turning down too many invitations because you have to meet a deadline or you are travelling. Or when you decide not to invest time and energy in a place because you won't be there long, if you live with your suitcase only partially unpacked. Is the situation an excuse to avoid commitment? Expatriates, humanitarian workers or the military or diplomatic service are particularly susceptible to this.

Beverley's professional activity in the US military allowed her to develop a pattern of moving from country to country and avoiding being tied down. She got engaged young but felt trapped.

I was so terrified of marrying my fiancé that I got out of it. After him, I had lots of different boyfriends and lots of frustrations. Either I wasn't interested and the boyfriend was or I was and he wasn't. Plus I was in the US military so either they would leave or I would. I never tried to stay to make relationships work.

After years of not being able to attach to a partner because of her travels, all changed in her early 50s on her first evening at a new posting.

Ahmed was the desk clerk at billeting. I had just arrived on the base in Turkey, he was on duty. I needed to call my brother to let him know I had arrived safely. This required a special phone card which I didn't have. Ahmed gave me his and showed me how to use it. He liked me immediately and I thought he had a magic touch with the phone. I had just gotten there from Italy, wasn't looking great I didn't think, although one of the guys said, "Hey go for her."

He was so cute, he had the most gentle eyes I'd ever seen. It was only a short interaction but I did think that he was so young.

In spite of Beverley's a priori that Ahmed, at more than 20 years her junior, was too young, it didn't stop the mutual attraction between the two:

Monday 5 am he was at the door to say I'd had a phone call and that he'd arranged for the caller to phone back. He took me to the billeting office so that I could get my call. We talked till my sister in law called back. After my conversation, he put me in a taxi to take me back to my room and paid for it.

Before I left the Base, I went to thank him and pay him back for the taxi. He wouldn't take the money, and was amazed that I was already leaving Turkey; he had wanted to take me out and show me the country.

I said, "How about tonight?"

This was something I had never done before. We went out with another couple and talked. He walked me back to my room and gave me his name and telephone number.

My mother always said, "Never let a man know you like him because it'll scare him away."

This time she was wrong because Ahmed says he was attracted by my saying that I liked him. I called him when I got back to Italy. He said he was missing me which blew me away. I left for the States, and could hardly wait to get there to have the photo of him developed so that I could see this cute guy who was missing me. After four weeks, I returned to Italy and called him. That's when our phone calls started, we must have talked for hours on the phone. I was getting really interested but as a marriage councillor I thought it was nuts because of the difference of age, religion, culture, and education. For example, I have a Ph.D., he'd never been to college.

In spite of these differences, Beverley decided she wanted to give this man a try:

I decided he needed to see my world and so I invited him to come to Italy. It was his first trip out of Turkey and we had a great time. He had wisdom far beyond his years. On his return to Turkey, I found him withdrawn. I was afraid this was going nowhere. A week later he called me and I sensed he was reluctant to leave his country. I went back to visit him and started to think about moving to Turkey. On my last night, he introduced me to his family. I felt like a 16-year-old kid I was so nervous, but I made a good impression. I had begun looking for a job on the base, and shortly after heard that I had been hired.

Beverley made another move, but this time to follow her heart:

This meant leaving a fantastic job in Italy to follow my heart for the first time in my life. I told Ahmed that I was taking a chance and of course he assured me that he would never let me down. I drove to Turkey and met him at the border. His family helped me to get settled. We lived together for about a year.

At the end of the year, I took him for Thanksgiving to my brother's house in the States. I knew that even if it didn't work out between us it would be so much fun giving him this opportunity.

The couple has been married near to 20 years. Beverley has stopped running and committed to a man who is different to her in age, religion, culture and education.

Exercise 5

Recognising your patterns, taking responsibility for your relationships and holding realistic expectations will help you to find and maintain a relationship, if you really want one. You might be finding, as you work through this first Step, that there are other areas in your life that could be impacting on your relationships. Is your life nicely balanced in all areas except one, or could you do with revamping several of them and making changes in different places?

The wheel of life exercise developed by the Co-Active Coaching Institute can help you to look at just where you are in your life right now. What needs fixing and what doesn't. I like to use it twice in my workshops for singles, before and after visualization.

It goes like this. Begin by drawing a circle and dividing it into eight sections. Label them romance, career, money, health, friends/family, personal growth, fun/recreation, home environment.

Note your level of satisfaction with each section by giving it a number from 1 to 10, with 10 being the highest. For example if you really enjoy your work you might give it a 10. Perhaps you are sharing a flat and don't like your flatmates' habit of eating your food without replacing it. As you are not totally happy with your home environment, you might only give it a 3.

When you have attributed the numbers, join them up across the sections. Look at how each is linked to the next. Does it flow from 10 to 10 or jump from 9 to 3? If this was the wheel of your car or bike, how smooth or bumpy a ride you would be giving yourself?

Figure 1 shows a wheel where every section has been given an 8. Although not perfect, the rider has a smooth ride.

When you have finished the exercise take 20 minutes to relax, or meditate or listen to a piece of music. If you decided to listen to music you could try a Prelude by Bach, a Mozart sonata or Rachmaninoff's piano concerto no. 2 or any other

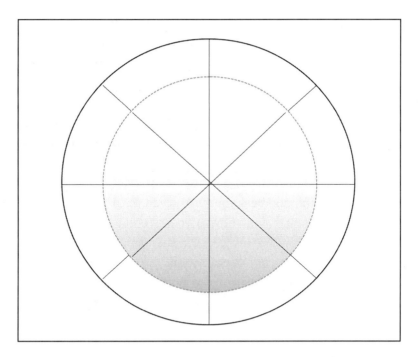

Figure 1 *Source: 2 Relationship Success*

music that resonates for you.

If you prefer a relaxation technique, here is one to try:

Locate a place where you won't be disturbed for at least 20 minutes. Close the door, switch off the phone and the computer. Seated in a comfortable chair, take three deep breaths, in through your nose, out through your mouth, with your eyes closed if that feels comfortable for you. At the same time count down 3,2,1, slowly, visualizing the numbers in descending order as you do it.

In your mind, you cross over a bridge with a small stream flowing beneath it. On the other side, you find a path leading into a beautiful garden. A striped deckchair is open welcomingly at just the right height. You sit down and look around, taking in the scented air, the birdsong and the warm sun on your skin.

When you feel comfortable and ready, visualize the eight

sections of your wheel of life one at a time. Imagine your professional life, how comfortable you are with it, your co-workers, the atmosphere and your salary. Go through all eight sections in the same way, thinking about the numbers that you gave them as you go along. Do they still reflect reality? Perhaps you are less happy in your professional life than you thought but your flat has a wonderful view that makes up for the flatmates.

Take at least 20 minutes to do this visualization. When you are satisfied with the numbers you have given each section, get up out of the deckchair and retrace your steps back through the garden and across the bridge. On the count of 1,2,3 bring yourself back out of your visualization.

Now redraw your wheel of life and fill in your satisfaction level for each part. Look at the circle and compare it to your previous drawing. What do you notice?

- Is there a good balance between the sections?
- Which sections, if any, have you changed since the visual-ization process?
- Which are the areas that you now need to work on?
- Look for links between the sections. For example if you have a high score on fun and recreation how could you use these activities to build up your social contacts?

Rethink your space, relook your home

By your 40s, you have established how much space you need to feel comfortable. You have your routines. You have acquired habits and behaviours that suit you and that you enjoy. Are you ready to share your own personal space?

Space can also refer to how close, emotionally, you wish to get to another person. Do you like to keep your distance, not get too close to a partner, or indeed anyone else for that matter? The next three stories concern singles who discuss their space issues.

You might find yourself so protective of it that you put up defences you are not even aware of. When I was single, I had a Yorkshire terrier called Bumble who I loved dearly. When he died one of my closest friends, and witness at my marriage, said that now that Bumble was no longer there I was free to meet a human partner. Bumble was protecting me from getting involved with the wrong person. To this day my husband thanks my little dog, though he never knew him, for making sure no one else got close before he did.

Lucy's story

Lucy's father was loving but distant. He suffered from depression and was lost in his own world. She had to work very hard to get his attention. According to Harville Hendrix in his book *Getting the love you want*, it was more than likely that this childhood experience would lead her to be attracted to distant men, those who worked long and hard at the office and were away playing competitive sports at the weekend. He explains how Lucy played out these childhood needs in adulthood, hoping unconsciously that this time she could heal the pain, that the grown up would rescue the child.

I had almost a sixth sense for the type of man who would not be available for me, who would let me down. Show me a hard working lawyer who spent all night in his office, or a sky diving enthusiastic who would jump off cliffs all weekend and I'd be after him, convinced that he was just what I wanted. When I was alone in the evenings or at weekends, I assured myself that I had the best of both worlds. I had a partner, but I also protected my space. I brushed the loneliness aside.

Hamish's story

Parents can be literally absent, as in the case of children who are sent young to boarding school. A child who is sent away is forced to grow up quickly and then spends the rest of their lives trying to get back what they missed. Well into his 30s, Hamish travelled the world with his bunny and teddy bear tucked away in his suitcase. He had been sent to boarding school aged 6 and had never quite recovered from that early parental separation. He married in his early 40s, when his girlfriend of three months fell pregnant. The two hardly knew each other. They had not learnt to share their space in spite of the initial desire for a child. He claims:

At boarding school I was forced to grow up too soon, to share my space like it or not. It took a long time to reach maturity.

Thierry's story

Thierry, a 47-year-old Parisian bachelor who has never married and intends to stay single, makes no bones about his need for space:

My last relationship lasted for nine years. It worked well while I was away in San Francisco for five months and at home in Paris for seven. However when a back operation forced me to stay in bed in Paris for a year, my live-in relationship stopped working. Suddenly the seven month here, five month there schedule was grounded with disastrous consequences for us. I am convinced that had we not been forced to spend the whole year in the same space we would still be together.

Space is not the only reason that Thierry doesn't want to commit. His reasons might be familiar to you too:

Firstly, life commitment is not for me, I've seen too many marriages fail. Secondly, I avoid legal commitments because it saves money if the relationship breaks up. Thirdly, I enjoy solitude and being alone, reading, though I am very sociable. Finally, I can't project into the future, I live in the present. I have nothing against marriage and kids for other people, just not for me. I hate routine. It kills relationships.

Exercise 6

Now it's your turn. How do you protect your space? You might get some surprising answers by glancing around you. In this exercise you are going to look at your home as a potential love nest for your couple, taking some tips from feng shui, the ancient Chinese art of placement.

If you have been living in your home for a while, you probably take your surroundings for granted. They could be saying the opposite to what you intend them to say. It's time to take stock; with pen and paper in hand, walk from room to room, beginning with the entrance.

The entrance and hall
- Is the front door clearly marked?
- Is it well lit?
- How do you feel as you enter the hall?
- Is there room to step inside?
- Are you greeted by a pile of clutter blocking your path?

The living room
- How welcoming is this room to guests?
- Are your photos mainly of you or friends on their own? How about adding some of couples and groups with you, laughing and enjoying yourselves?
- What of the pictures? Again are they of single figures or groups?
- Is the furniture arranged in a cosy, comfortable group or are there straight-backed, isolated chairs dotted around?

The bedroom
- Do you have a single bed? Where will you and your partner sleep?
- Is there a bedside table and lamp on either side of the bed?

Eating arrangements
- Do you have more than one chair at your breakfast table?
- Are there enough knives and forks, glasses and plates for two of you?

The cupboards
- Is there room for someone else's clothes and belongings?
- Will you ever wear all those clothes or it is time to give some away?

The verdict

Ask a good friend, preferably one in a stable relationship, to visit and give you an honest appraisal of your home as an outsider seeing it for the first time.

Focus on these adjustments and you will feel the energy beginning to shift in your home. You might find that you can't wait to show off your new acquisitions. Someone has to try out that new sofa or dining room chairs. You are focussing on what you want, allowing it to come into your life. Sit down in your nice comfortable rearranged seat. There is just one more exercise to do before you move outside.

Exercise 7
Draw your treasure map

The work that you have done in this chapter has helped you to look at possible obstacles to happiness; it has made you focus on what you are looking for in your relationships and elsewhere in your life. You are going to take it a step further by drawing a treasure map which will help to make it tangible. If you have done this exercise before, do it this time with your newfound knowledge of your heart's desire.

Take a large coloured piece of cardboard. Choose a colour that resonates with you. It can be A4 or larger, as big as possible. Then take some magazines and flip through them, cutting out any of the photos that appeal to you and that represent your future life with your partner. Do you want to go on golfing holidays together, ride horses, live in a castle, dance till dawn, eat croissants and drink coffee as the sun rises or smell the roses in an English garden? Find photos that illustrate your dreams and cut them out. Put the photos aside. When you have a good pile, paste them onto your piece of board in any way that looks harmonious to you. Finish your collage with a photo of yourself in the centre. Write an affirmation such as Shakti Gawain's from her book, *Creative Visualization*:

> "This or something better now manifests for me in totally satisfying and harmonious ways, for the highest good of all concerned" or
> "I now have total intention to create this here and now."

Have fun with the treasure map and open your mind to possibility. Remember the affirmation has to resonate with you.

When you are satisfied with the results of the exercises that you have completed in this Step, you are ready to move on to Step Two and Out into the World.

In Step One you looked at:
- How to take responsibility in your relationships.
- How to become the chooser not the chosen and to take ownership of your decisions.
- Your expectations, keeping them high but still realistic.
- Your must-haves, once again with a dose of realism.
- Problematic relationship patterns. They included falling for the same style of person who does not suit you and avoiding commitment.
- Where you are in your life at the moment in all areas, not just relationships.
- Your home and whether it is welcoming to a new partner and opportunities.
- Your treasure map showing your goals in words and pictures.

Step Two:
Out into the World, Initial Success

You have heeded The Call; you are now ready to go Out into the World. Make use of the new perspective that you have acquired since overcoming some of the issues that were holding you back. In this Step you could well meet a Prince or Princess, outshining your rivals in the process. Tread carefully along your chosen path for all is not yet clear.

Step Two will help you to:

- *Get rid of limiting beliefs*
- *Do things differently*
- *Identify meeting places that work such as: professional meetings, relocation, classes, introductions through friends, the Internet*
- *Check your Internet profile*
- *Look at dating agencies.*

In the first Step of your journey to meeting and keeping your partner, you looked at the issues that had blocked you in the past. You identified thoughts and actions that had prevented you from living a stable relationship. In the process, you gained an understanding of issues that have proven to be obstacles.

You are now clearer about your objectives. Nevertheless you could still be hanging on to some limiting beliefs that are hampering your progress and making you feel powerless to change anything.

Get rid of limiting beliefs

"Reality is a projection of your thoughts or the things you habitually think about."
Stephen Richards

Cognitive behavioural therapists emphasize that it is not an event, but thoughts about the event that influence feelings that in turn influence behaviours. Imagine you are reading a book on a subject that you don't know much about. Do you think to yourself that it is badly written and hardly surprising that you can't understand a word of it? Or do you instead think that it is your fault for not understanding and how stupid you are? You will feel different depending on which of these views you adopt. Your reaction or behaviour in each case will also be influenced. Our thoughts, feelings and behaviour are interlinked. Each affects the other. Some of the phrases listed below can have a powerful negative effect on your feelings that then influences your behaviour. They need to be taken with a grain of salt.

1. I never meet the right person

"There is nothing sweeter than finding the right person to love and cherish and to share your hopes and dreams with."
Mary Lydon Simonsen, *The Perfect Bride for Mr Darcy*

Research carried out by the Swiss Parcours de Vie Institute shows that the right person is likely to be someone very much like you. Like tends to stick to like when it comes to choosing a life partner, e.g. you look for someone with similar tastes, education, profession, even looks in some cases. The prince who falls in love with the shepherdess is not as common as television sitcoms would have you believe.

The good news is that your match could be just round the corner, in the supermarket, at your local sports club or at an evening class, doing the sort of things you like to do.

Esther and Tom's story
Both single and in their early 40s, Esther and Tom, were committee members at their local squash club. They had known

each for 14 years before Tom asked Esther to the cinema after an evening committee meeting. Then it was dinner and soon one thing led to another. They met through their common passion for squash, enjoyed sports and cared enough about the club and fundraising to give up their free time to sit on the committee. They were two like-minded souls, even if it took them 14 years to realize that the right person was sitting on the other side of the table.

2. All the good ones are taken

Interesting research carried out by French business school INSEAD and published in the Journal of Psychological Science, found that humans put more value on what is rare and difficult to attain. They tested the hypothesis by getting men and women to view the same number of photographs of attractive and less attractive people.

When questioned later, both men and women believed that there were fewer attractive people of the opposite sex than there were of the same sex, in spite of the fact that the number of photos of men and women was identical. Participants believed that what they wanted, that is an attractive partner, was less available. When the portraits were unattractive, they no longer felt the same sense of scarcity. If you think that all the good ones are taken, it might be your sense of scarcity talking.

By your 40s and beyond, you have probably had several relationships. So has the man or woman that you are looking for. Just like you, at some stage they too will separate from their partner. They will be in between relationships. The key is to be there when they too are looking for someone new.

Nevertheless, facts are facts. In the US there are 30 million single women over 40 and 20 million single men. That is a fact. There are 15 million singles in the UK between the ages of 18 and 64 and more than half of them are looking for a stable relationship. No matter what the figures say, you personally are only looking for one person, the right person… And you can find them no matter how stacked the odds are against you.

Lily's story

Blonde, single mother Lily in her mid-50s attended a professional women's speed networking event with only a handful of men present. The odds were 60-5 and yet she still met her match. If you haven't tried it, professional speed networking is like speed dating but with a professional objective, which takes off some of the pressure.

> We had two minutes to tell our story to someone in the room. We explained what we did and what we were looking for professionally. When the bell rang, we'd hand over our business cards and move on to the next person and begin again. I had recently left my job and was looking for freelance editing, not for a partner. Nevertheless I noticed this tall, handsome man immediately, but I was sure that he was collecting business cards for his professional use only.
>
> Tall and slim with beautiful blue eyes and slender hands, he was impeccably dressed in a dark suit - and a perfectly knotted blue silk tie! Then I heard his voice - gentle and melodious and without any hint of an accent. He was very attentive and well-mannered and had a wicked sense of humour. He made me feel special.

It didn't take long for her to realize she'd struck gold:

> My heart was a-flutter, my feet didn't touch the ground, I couldn't take my eyes off him, all the corny things. I'd never known such an overwhelming feeling of happiness and hoped it would never end. Ours was a case of serendipity. I couldn't believe it when he called me the next day to invite me out.
>
> I think the timing was key as both of us were in other relationships for most of our adult lives until that point so we would not have been searching for a partner.

77

Lily's encounter through speed networking is in stark contrast to Lori Gottlieb's unhappy experience with speed dating in *Marry Him: The Case for Settling for Mr. Good Enough*. Gottlieb tells how, aged 41, she had signed up for the 40-50 age group. Surprise No. 1: when she got to the trendy restaurant where the event was taking place, she saw that there were ten single women for only six available men.

> *I checked out the six men. Surprise No. 2: all but one looked older than 50, and one guy looked so old that he bore a striking resemblance to my best friend's father... So there we were: eight early-fortyish women, two late-fortyish women, one mid-fortyish man, and five men over 50.*

3. There are not enough ways and places to meet where I live

Even if you live in a small town, there are activities available. Professional luncheons, after work drinks and breakfasts, are popular. The choice is vast. By carefully organising your agenda, you can have lunch with a different group almost every day of the week. There is a lot of eating and drinking involved, but it is still a good way of broadening your horizons. If you want to circulate and not get stuck with two neighbours for an entire lunch, you are probably better to stick to after work drinks.

"People just want to meet new people, to network," said the organiser of a Swiss Canadian networking event. He should know, the ground floor of his law firm offices was packed with professional men and women sharing business cards, experiences and perhaps more besides.

Exercise 1

Are there associations that you have thought of joining and either never got around to exploring or just decided that they were probably not for you? Even if you have done this exercise before, try it one more time. This time could be the right one.

- Begin by identifying your interests. Divide into professional, personal development and sports and leisure activities.
- Choose a favourite from each and research the associations and clubs available on that subject.
- Identify one of their events that you will attend by a particular deadline.
- Enlist a friend's help to keep you to your deadline, or even to go with you.

An example of taking up a new activity could be joining a class, for example, a dance class. There is something about dancing classes. More of my respondents met through dance classes than any other non-professional activity. Perhaps it is the initial pairing up, the romance and seduction of the movements and the harmony of the music.

Amongst the dance class aficionados, single, early 40s Amanda met her partner, who is three years older, at a Tango class in Manchester. She had joined the class with the specific intention of meeting someone new and it worked for her.

Martina's story

Dancing classes also worked for American early 50s Martina who met her Dutch partner at a ballroom dancing class in the Netherlands where they lived. She was struck by his beautiful hands but did have two concerns:

He was too young! He's 10 years younger and he looks young for his age. And he's too short. We are the same height.

Martina had signed up for the classes because she was feeling unhappy and overwhelmed on professional and personal levels at the time. She took the dance class as stress relief.

I didn't think about a romantic attraction until after the class, when we started calling and emailing each other because we realized we missed our weekly time together and conversations after each lesson.

The two are still dancing, this time across the Atlantic to a new life in the US.

My husband and I are taking a big leap together, moving from his country to my country in stages. Stage 1 begins when I move back to the US and enrol for a 1-year course for a new skill set. He will follow sometime during the year, as he settles various things in the Netherlands, finds a new job and joins me. That all sounds fairly crazy, but we think it will work.

An attractive younger partner and a new life beginning in another country: Martina's story all began with one dance step.

4. I don't want to look desperate

This limiting belief is often heard in the company of its companion "What will people think?" Both can restrict your spontaneity and hamper you unnecessarily. Attracting someone into your life for more than friendship isn't an act of desperation – it's an act of self-love. You deserve a fulfilling partnership, and the first step of that process is meeting someone new.

It may seem obvious to you, but others might not be aware that you would like to meet someone. Let them know that you are looking. I don't mean whining to everyone who will listen, but just let it be known that you would like to meet someone new.

Exercise 2

Are you comfortable asking for help? Many of us are not, fearing rejection. And yet we are delighted to help when we are asked. Perhaps you fear that others will judge you, that they will see you as vulnerable, not as perfect as you would like.

If asking doesn't come naturally to you, begin flexing your asking-for-help muscle by practicing every day. Ask for directions in the street, the tomato ketchup from the next table in a restaurant or to open the window in the office. When you are at ease asking for small things, move on to those nearer to your heart. Above all don't be hard on yourself if you don't feel comfortable at your first attempt.

Anne's story

It worked for early 40s Anne, who had the courage to open her heart to a co-worker and friend with great results.

I'm a teacher. One day at work I was having lunch with a co-worker. He was a close friend and so I just blurted out that I needed a man to hug at the end of the day. My friend heard me loud and clear. He turned up with his best friend John's email the very next day.

I had tried lots of things before. I'd been to singles dances, dating websites and a dating service. Nothing came out of any of my attempts. I had also made a list of the qualities that I was looking for in a partner. With hindsight, it nicely corresponded to my partner. I was looking for someone with family values, who valued marriage and had not been married before. I found all of that.

5. I never meet anyone interesting, smart, sexy, single, or...

How true is that? Think about who you have met recently and compare them to your big five essential requirements from the last step. How do they look now? If they still don't match up, it's time to widen your horizons.

Do things differently

"Dating is probably the most fraught human interaction there is. You're sizing people up to see if they're worth your time and attention, and they're doing the same to you. It's meritocracy applied to personal life, but there's no accountability."
Adelle Waldman, *The love affairs of Nathaniel P*

Everyone who shares their story in this book has one key point in common.

They all changed something in their lives. For some it was a change in attitude, for others a step outside of their comfort zone, for a few recognition of what was blocking them, yet others travelled or moved and some signed up for courses. Shortly after becoming aware of the need for change and then putting it into practice, they met their partner.

In the first part of this book, I described how I met my husband in the desert on a study tour organised by the Rector of my local church. The trip featured nights in the open air in 0 degree temperatures with 15 complete strangers and no bathroom. It was like chalk to the cheese of my previous birthdays. But off I went and met my true love.

What could you do differently? You could begin by looking at meeting places with a new perspective. There are hidden treasures out there.

Identify the meeting places that work

When I was writing this book, the first page was read anonymously to Geneva writers and literary agents at a "Meet the agents" workshop. Along with some 30 other entries its fate was determined by whether the agents, seated on a podium, would ping the bell in front of them, signifying its elimination. I was one of the lucky three to be read to the very end. After I introduced myself several women in the audience came up to me to ask, "Where do you meet a man in Geneva?"

Geneva is a good case in point. It has been said that if you can meet someone here you can meet someone anywhere. My city of adoption is known for the United Nations, private banks and a notorious lack of available men – one to every eight women in some years. Not that men fare any better in an international community, in spite of the statistics. *"We are all from such different backgrounds, it is rare to meet someone that you can share a real complicity with,"* says American Bill, a cultured and much-travelled expatriate and long-term single (Complicity is discussed further in Step Three).

Like Bill, you may have already tried lots of places where you expect to meet someone new. Whether you are a newcomer in town or a long term resident, you have already visited many of the local watering holes. This time, however, your search is going to take on a new perspective, inspired by the experience of the couples that share their stories of finding love over 40.

The popularity of one type of meeting place over another has not changed much over the years, apart from the addition of online services. In 1994, *The Social Organization Of Sexuality: Sexual Practices In The United States*, by Edward O. Laumann, John H. Gagnon, Robert T. Michael and Stuart Michaels, found work and school to be the most common meeting places, between 15 and 20% of their respondents. In my survey nearly 20 years later, work associated events and education are still in the lead although Internet accounted for 30% of meetings.

Ways of meeting fall roughly into two categories. On the one hand, there is the traditional approach of introductions through friends or family, work-related activities or education and training. It can take time and be hard to instigate for newcomers to town, expatriates and workaholics. The other option is to take a pro-active role through the Internet, speed dating, dating agencies, love coaches and a myriad of specialists that have sprung up for this purpose. As you have bought this book you are already taking your destiny into your own hands. It will lead you to consider your options.

The professional meeting

Often, relationships between colleagues are frowned on. They can make the atmosphere uncomfortable if things don't work out. The embarrassing stories of a romantic email finding its way to the wrong recipient are legion. If you work in an all-female or all-male environment and are looking for a partner of the opposite sex, you are unlikely to find him/her at the next desk, although you might develop a strategy for it to happen. For example if you are secretary in an international women's club you might tell some of these women what you are looking for. Their husbands could have single colleagues.

The professional meeting therefore covers more than sharing the same office or working in the same company with a potential partner. I invite you to step outside of your office and attend some work-related events. As it is, a lot of your free time is probably taken up with these, many of them offering potentially fertile ground for meeting a partner.

Charlotte's story

Even the event you didn't really want to go to can come up trumps, as early 40s public relations specialist Charlotte discovered. Not long after she had moved to Richmond, Virginia, a younger colleague suggested they go to a networking meeting organised by two professional associations. Charlotte didn't yet know many people in the southern town and agreed to go in order to check out the two associations. Prepared to make some professional contacts, Charlotte was looking business-like in a cream coloured suit:

> *The event took place in a run down sports bar in Richmond. It was a straightforward networking social for business groups and local young professionals. I walked in with a friend and colleague who had talked me into joining her. I was new to town. My friend saw my future partner and marched me over to meet him because she thought we were closer in age and might hit it off.*

Charlotte was a new arrival in town. She was prepared to go to places she didn't know and was not influenced by whether an event sounded promising or not. If she had lived in Richmond for longer she would have known that this association was or was not for her and perhaps have missed the opportunity of an important meeting.

Relocation
Consuelo's story

Moving to a new town worked for advertising executive Consuelo when she engineered a transfer to a different office within the same company. She had spent the past few years heavily invested in her career, had gone back to university to get her MBA, was working full-time as well as caring for her ill mother. A relationship wasn't really on her mind.

This changed the day she woke up and thought,

I'd like to get married and I know that my future husband lives in Brooklyn.

Simple as that. Why Brooklyn? The name sounded romantic to Consuelo, a place for dreams, a place to find a husband.

My sister was already living in New York but that wasn't what I was looking for. I liked the comfort of knowing my postman, my neighbours, of living in the suburbs. Yet I kept really feeling my future partner was in that part of the world. I told my older divorced sister who thought it was a ridiculous idea. I didn't give up and travelled to New York for work to see if I liked it. I did.

With a swish of her long black hair, Consuelo focussed on her goal of moving to Brooklyn, asking God for help. Little by little a plan formed in her mind. Firstly she looked for all the information she could get about the Brooklyn office. Her agency had offices all over the US. Each local agency specialised in different accounts. Ohio promoted agricultural products, machinery and some crops like potatoes. Brooklyn promoted museums and the opera house. Consuelo thought of how she had done some voluntary work at the local community centre helping to promote amateur operatics.

I set up an appointment with my boss and told him how I felt it was time to move, to grow, particularly now that I had my MBA. I was looking for a new challenge… and besides I love the opera.

My boss was doubtful, he needed me in Ohio, I had run the farm equipment account for five years and he didn't want me to leave it. After all it was one of their biggest accounts. I kept pushing. I had just the person to take over my job. Initially I would come back regularly so as not to abandon the account. I just really wanted to make this move.

Finally my boss gave in. I must have been persuasive as he agreed to move me from Ohio and paid for the transfer.

Consuelo's strategy had worked. She was on her way to meet her future husband.

On my first day in Brooklyn I walked around the neighbourhood and saw a small Italian restaurant. The doors were open as it was summer. I walked by and saw him behind the counter. I did a double take. I thought, "He's cute" and walked back in the opposite direction to take a second look. I went in almost every day to order something. It took a while to get his attention. I saw he was always smiling, friendly, loved his work and knew it thoroughly. After some weeks he started talking to me then invited me for a drink. I could look down on where he worked from my new apartment. It was truly meant to be, some things are beyond my understanding.

The moment I saw him I thought that his heart was filled with goodness. He was happy, smiling and laughing whenever I saw him. He "looked like" my husband.

I can't say what that means. His heart seemed like the heart of a child, it seemed so pure. He had been brought up similar to the way I was raised. If someone needs something you share with him or her. Not many people are like that anymore. We enjoy doing things together too, he cooks and I love to cook so that is something that is really fun for us to do. It is a treat for him to eat the kind of food I cook coming from the Dominican Republic. We have also discovered music together.

Consuelo's plan took a while to put into place but she stuck to it, convinced she was doing the right thing. And her strategy paid off. Although a transfer within the company is not something that everyone can bring about, it is an example of getting out and going somewhere different, making a change. A change doesn't necessarily mean that you have to move to a new home. Here is an exercise that can help you to make a change by adding or subtracting something in your life.

Exercise 3

Science has proven that 30 days is all it takes to reprogramme the brain. Take advantage of this by incorporating something new into your life every day. You will discover that within 30 days you have accomplished something you set your heart on and perhaps never thought you could do or simply never got around to doing. This is how it works.

Get into a comfortable position, somewhere where you won't be disturbed. Close your eyes and relax your body completely, muscle by muscle, beginning with your toes, feet, legs and up through your body to the top of your head. Count down from ten to one, breathing deeply and feeling more and more relaxed with each count. When you are ready, start to visualize something that you would really like to do.

Imagine as clearly as possible, adding all your senses to the picture. Perhaps you want to write a novel, knit a sweater or run a marathon. If you want to write a novel, what will the jacket cover look like, how will the fresh pages feel in your hands? If you want to knit a sweater, how silky or rough will it feel, what colours will you choose?

If you want to run a marathon, how tired are the muscles of your legs after your first practice run? How long did it take you?

Go into more detail as you imagine what it will take to achieve your goal in 30 days. For example if you decide to write a novel you need to identify how many words it will contain and for how long you are going to write every day, if you want to run a marathon, how much practice you can fit in. If you have decided to knit a sweater, who will wear it, how does he/she look wearing it?

The other option is to subtract something from your life instead of adding. That is remove something that is damaging to you. For example, you might decide to cut down on your sugar intake. Ask yourself how much you will reduce daily before you cut it out completely. Do you usually take sugar in coffee or add it to yogurt? See yourself spooning in less, taste the drink or food, enjoy it without the sugar. As ever, be as precise as possible with your visualisation.

There are various benefits to doing this exercise. Firstly of course you will achieve something that you hadn't thought you could do. This gives you a new motivation day by day to carry on with your activity as you see it develop. In addition your self-confidence will grow as you see what you can do. You can give yourself a new title with each new achievement.

If you want to choose a goal related to your search for a partner you might try connecting with someone new every day for 30 days. This will keep you focussed.

Exercise 4

Giving either by attending an event or taking a more active role such as volunteering as a fund-raiser is a great way of meeting new people and feeling good about yourself in the process.

Identify a cause that you would like to become involved with and offer your time to its development. Follow the instructions given for Exercise 1.

Nilufar's story

Jordanian-born philanthropist and diplomat's daughter Nilufar goes to a lot of fund-raising events and expects to be comfortable when she gets there. This is how she met her husband James:

I went to a fund-raising event with my mother and we found ourselves in an over-crowded box at the Royal Albert Hall. To get some space we moved to the next box where James was sitting by himself.

I wasn't thinking that I was about to meet my future husband, neither before the evening nor after I had met James. In fact it was my mother who asked for his card and invited him over when she needed a man to make up the numbers.

It wasn't love at first sight. James came for dinner twice before he asked me out. We went out for months on and off with neither of us revealing what we were really thinking. It wasn't until after at least five months of these evenings that the masks fell and James and I began to talk in earnest. We were in his car. We talked and talked until 5 in the morning. Finally I saw the real James behind the shy widower.

I believe in fate. If it is meant to be it will be, usually when you least expect it to happen. If it's meant to be you will be where you have to be.

Nilufar in her 50s was not looking for a partner in particular, but her generosity for causes led her to him.

Classes
Alfred's story

Universities and technical colleges are increasingly accessible to mature students as they aim to encourage diversity in the student body. Further education provides the opportunity to up your qualifications and to meet people with similar interests and ambitions. Who knows, you might change more than your curriculum vitae like Alfred and Luisa.

Alfred is an American lawyer. He had never been married

before he met Luisa. He was in his late 40s at the time. Luisa was a mature student from Colombia, some 14 years his junior. She had travelled half way round the world to get the best training available in her chosen area of trade law. Geographically worlds apart, the two nevertheless had common ground to build their relationship.

Luisa stood out from the crowd with her beautiful smile and dark eyes. We started talking in the coffee break at a tall table in a cafeteria in Switzerland's capital city. We discussed the difficulties of leaving our respective countries, Colombia and America, and leaving our family and friends at home. We had no idea that this meeting would be significant but the seeds were sown.

Both were united by their mutual interest in a particular branch of the law, an interest that had motivated them to travel round the world and seek out the best.

Jenny's story

In the 1994 study carried out by Laumann, Gagnon, Michael and Michaels that I mentioned earlier, the authors discovered that churches were good for meeting marriage partners (11%), and not surprisingly poor for meeting short-term sex partners (1%). When you meet a man or woman at church or synagogue, you know you have a potential alliance with someone who shares your religious values. Most churches encourage fellowship by organizing social and volunteer opportunities that are open to new members. They are particularly useful for newcomers and expatriates where they can serve as a good entry into the local community.

Early 40s Filipino statistician Jenny had lived in New York before moving to Bangkok. On arrival she joined her local church. Soon she met and fell in love with the Rector. Jenny didn't jump into marriage. She asked God for guidance and thought about her decision for some while. Today she couldn't be happier with the outcome. She tells of other members of her church throughout the world whose members of all ages have met life partners.

Introductions through friends

If you have lived in the same town for some time you may well have friends who as we have seen can be instrumental in introducing you to others. Even here, a change is possible by trying a different place or accepting that uninspiring dinner.

In this section on meeting through friends, I would like you to imagine that you are at a dinner party with a group of people who all met and married, many of them for the first time, over 40. They are going to share their stories.

Kevin's story

Late 30s mother of two, Samantha was interested in meeting local Geneva radio presenter Kevin and had asked a friend to set up a meeting. The friend suggested they meet at the Pickwick pub, a popular expatriate hangout, and much beloved by 40-something never married Kevin.

Kevin's view of marriage was that it *"boxed you in."* He protected himself by going out with much younger girls, girls who were not looking for commitment.

Samantha did not usually go to pubs by herself but nevertheless agreed to her friend's suggestion. It was she, rather than Kevin, who had stepped outside of her comfort zone in order to meet him. Kevin remembers that he hadn't made any effort on the clothing score. He was dressed for a business meeting that he had attended earlier:

This was not the first time I had agreed to meet someone who wanted to meet me. She said she had children so I assumed she was married. We met at the right moment for part of me had changed; I was open to changing my life and being more serious. We got on well, had a few drinks, possibly too many. It was all very pleasant. Samantha didn't go to bars often as she has children. I was struck by how different she was to other women I had met.

Our relationship began on slow burn. We arranged to meet later and slowly became more serious about each other. Timing is every-thing. I was in the frame of mind to change my life and she was too.

Giancarlo's story

Friends played an unintentional role when Giancarlo met his partner at a relaxed dinner for six in the home of a mutual friend. It was an informal evening and the Swiss decorator was not expecting anything more than an enjoyable time with friends over drinks and nibbles.

I had already spotted her in the street and thought that she was beautiful. She had also seen me earlier flirting with a girl on a scooter. She found my behaviour seductive. We mixed in the same circle of friends so it was probably only a question of time before we actually met up.

As the night drew in beyond the cocktail hour, it wasn't long before he had his arm around her.

I sat in an armchair, she was at my feet. I put my hand on her neck and that was it.

Barbara's story

You might expect your friends to come up with useful contacts and introductions; it is more unexpected to meet a potential partner through your current partner. This is what happened to Barbara when she met her future husband from Australia through her then partner who worked with him.

Initially our then partners who worked together introduced us. We all had brunch together and I knew, looking at him that there was something wrong with this picture. I was dating the wrong man.

For Barbara it was love at first sight:

Even though we were both "otherwise engaged" I could not get this man out of my mind – even though I didn't know if I would ever see him again. When I saw him a year later, I once again recognised him as being mine immediately. His strength of character, honour and self-knowledge shone through... and I felt like I was glowing whenever I was near him.

We probably would not have even dated each other had we met in our twenties. We had to grow into the people we were meant to be before we could be together... and yes, the people we are definitely were, and are, meant to be together. We haven't been apart since we met up a year after that brunch.

Exercise 5

Here is an exercise to help you make the most of your friends and network.

Chances are that many of your friends are single. Pool your resources by organising a party where each person invites someone of the opposite sex that no one else knows. This can be a challenge in a small town, but is always fun. Alternatively you could try something on a smaller scale like a dinner party. Ask a friend of the opposite sex to invite two others that you don't know while you invite two people that he/she doesn't know. This exercise will enable you to meet a lot of new people, make new friends and enjoy yourself in the process.

The Internet

In the UK, singles aged 55 and older are the most active online daters according to research carried out for the Daily Telegraph's Stella magazine. Findings reveal that 62% of respondents have used a dating site and have gone out on an average of 8.2 dates and had 2.1 long-term relationships. This is borne out by research at Iowa State University which found in a study of 175 newlywed couples that those who met through social networking or online dating sites tended to be older than those who met without the help of the Internet. They were also more likely to be on their second marriage. The courtship for couples that met through the Internet also tended to be much shorter at 18.5 months, when compared to 42 months for a relationship brought about by other means.

While one in five US singles claims to have tried an on line-dating agency, it is not so simple to get it right as you saw from Susanne's story in Step One (see page 49). There are other things to keep in mind too.

Check your Internet profile
Philippe's story

Early 50s Philippe met his love when a thoughtful friend opened an account for him with an Internet dating site. Philippe had suffered a painful break up and his friend wanted to point him in the direction of a fresh start. His story brings to light the importance of writing a clear profile, and getting the details straight.

After months of reading boring profiles that all sounded alike, Philippe decided to give the site one last try on his son's birthday, 22 October. When he logged on, the first profile he came to was Celine's. He was impressed with her clarity; she seemed to know exactly what she wanted. Unlike other profiles, her page was not cluttered with *"looking for prince charming"* or *"a serious man"*. Instead she insisted on her own failings, what she was looking for, her love of fine restaurants and her likes and dislikes. When Philippe answered her, she replied smartly that she was not in his age group. It turned out that Philippe's well-intentioned friend had indicated that he was looking for a girl of 20-30. Philippe immediately changed his criteria to 0-77 and fixed a meeting with Celine. Philippe claims that he has never been happier since marrying Celine. The two laugh together about the age misunderstanding over dinners in romantic restaurants.

Jessica's story

Jessica met her partner through friends of friends' profiles on Facebook, which was new at the time. She attributes the ease of their meeting to their openness with each other on the social media site.

Leo is Australian and was living in Turkey. I was in New Zealand, my home. We started messaging and chatting, not thinking we'd ever meet. We were very open with each other, revealing a lot of things. He was finalizing his divorce and he wasn't working so he had the time to message me. I was at home with little to do too and wasn't feeling particularly happy. Normally I wouldn't admit that I was unhappy to a complete stranger, I tend to pretend everything is great. Perhaps because we didn't think we'd meet we were very open with each other. We got on well, which didn't stop me getting annoyed when I didn't hear from him.

After some months, Leo emailed to say he was coming home to Australia. I suggested we meet up but didn't hear till two days before I was due to leave Sydney as he got his dates mixed up. Nevertheless we still managed to meet for lunch. Our meeting was very easy; he was kind, with a gentle energy. I wasn't in the least uptight about meeting him in person for the first time. When he walked in it felt like I knew him, it just all seemed to click. We'd seen photos of each other and he looked just like his photo. With hindsight I can see that we had a real friendship established. I felt I could be myself. I was relaxed around him. We laughed a lot. We're so well suited, people comment on it. He has a huge capacity to love.

Everything moved fast after that first meeting in Sydney, perhaps because they had got to know each other online.

> *I suggested he come to the wedding of my Greek neighbours in New Zealand. I'd gone as a single women to the previous weddings in that family and each time older family members would come up to me saying, "What's a pretty young woman like you doing alone?"*
>   *I decided next time I'd go with someone.*
>   *Leo came for a week and stayed for two. He had a trip to Thailand booked. Of course I drove him to the airport. We hadn't made any plans. At the airport he asked me, "Shall I come back?" When I said yes, I knew that it meant his living with me.*

Leo did come back, did a cooking course in Christchurch and the couple, now married continue to travel the world together.

The dating agency

If the Internet is not your thing, there is the dating agency option. I spoke to Trea Tijmens, who runs Success Match, Switzerland's biggest dating agency and matchmaking service to find out what clients can expect from this type of service. In fact there are two services, one more personalised than the other. They allow Trea to identify the perfect partner, she claims. This is based on in-depth meeting and some psychological testing. Apparently the success rate is hard to quantify as once a client has found a partner they tend not to be heard from again. It is only those that don't work out who go back to the service for another introduction. To find out how it went, Trea runs an evaluation of the first date. It seems that 95% of clients are satisfied or even extremely satisfied with their first date and 70% are prepared to meet the person again. What about the third date I wondered? It is often around date number three that serious questions start to arise.

Success Match appeals in particular to busy expatriates who are finding that they have a lack of opportunity to meet someone new or they are meeting lots of people but not the right one, people with different expectations and goals for the future. They don't want to waste time and so entrust their future relationship happiness to a dating agency.

In Step Two you looked at taking a different approach to your way of meeting someone. In particular you looked at:

- Getting rid of limiting beliefs that hamper your search.
- Doing things differently like others interviewed in this book. Not dramatically different, just different.
- Identifying meeting places that work such as: Professional meetings, Relocation, Classes, Introductions through friends, the Internet.
- Checking your Internet profile to be sure it is fresh and appealing, reflecting what you really want.
- Dating agencies.

Step Three:
The Central Crisis

Step Three is about meeting someone new and taking the relationship from first meetings to the first few months. It looks at whether the relationship has potential, whether it is worth pursuing and what you can do differently this time.

Possibly you have just met someone and are opening this book at Step Three because you are not sure about your new relationship. Understandably you are cautious, this where it's gone wrong in the past. This Step is called the Central Crisis. It can lead either to a false start or a happy end. It covers:

- *First few meetings: Internet or face-to-face*
- *Give it a chance*
- *What was different this time?*
- *Compatibility in the first few months: if you clicked it could be wrong*
- *Attachment styles: secure and insecure*

And yet so blind is love that defects often seem to be virtues, deformity assumes the style of beauty, and even hideous vices have appeared under an attractive form.
Edward John Hardy. *How to be happy though married*

The first few meetings: Internet or face-to-face

So here you are, having followed the advice in the previous Steps and been on a date or two. You're not sure what to think. Your heart didn't beat faster, in fact you were put off by the way the person was dressed or their choice of venue. Just remain curious and keep an open mind. Some people seem unpromising when you first meet them and yet they blossom on a later date. Others make you feel great but with hindsight the person is not really right for you.

In this Step you are going to learn how the relationships developed for the couples whose stories you discovered in the last two Steps. Some hit it off quickly, others did not. Nearly all took their time to get to know each other, whether over the Internet or in person. All are together, happily, today.

First meetings are brought about in one of two ways: they are planned or unplanned. In the first case scenario you officially meet each other through a source such as the Internet, the classifieds or a dating agency. You already know a little about each other if you've both been truthful. You have been able to prepare yourself for a face-to-face meeting, find out a bit about the person you are going to meet, discover what you have in common and perhaps take some psychological tests that indicate you are a good match. On the plus side, you are prepared for the meeting. On the negative side your expectations can be high and disappointment can ensue if the person doesn't come up to scratch.

In the second case scenario you meet directly in person by chance or by arrangement. You know nothing about each other, unless it is a blind date, and you have only chemistry and gut-feelings to go on. There are no expectations if it's a surprise meeting.

Before you read about those first meetings and think about your own, how about trying an activity to open your heart, like Jessica from New Zealand who met her husband on Facebook:

I started Anusara yoga which is about opening your heart, opening to something bigger, grace. I met my partner shortly after I began this new practice.

1. The Internet

The Internet has a lot in its favour. The dating agency has already done a pre-selection and given you an indication that this person could be right for you. Don't leave it too long before you meet though. Recent research shows that online communications can take on their own existence over time, filling a need. When the couple finally meet up they miss that regular screen-to-screen communication and can even start looking for a replacement Internet contact.

Susanne's story 2

Susanne and Paul agreed to get together in person a week after their first online contact (Step One, see page 49). Susanne had enlarged her profile requirements and had almost immediately met Paul. She felt relaxed as she looked forward to their date because of the good contact that had been established:

I didn't feel any butterflies.

If anyone had said to me at the end of that first evening, "This is the guy you're going to marry in less than a year's time," I would have said, "I don't think so."

He was a nice guy and it was a pleasant evening but nothing more. It took another two or three dates first. I warmed to him slowly, but surely.

Susanne felt that there had been a shift along with her change of profile. Something was different:

Mainly my own attitude... I remembered his words about love, our high correspondence on the Internet test and the Internet agency recommendation to meet up at least a second time even if you dislike each other completely. So I consciously decided to be patient, to take it slowly, to stick with it for a while and to see what might come of it.

Paul was grown-up and mature. According to the dating site's psychological test he was a good match for me that's why I chose to contact him, especially given his sweet sentence about love, which corresponds with my own view.

Because the two had already met over the Internet they had some idea what to expect. They also had the results of the online psychological test which were favourable. They liked each other but were not expecting miracles.

First time online daters might like to know that Susanne had been given some general advice on how to dress. The dating agency recommended that she wear casual clothes for the first date, only dressing up for subsequent dates, if there are subsequent dates. In Susanne's case of course there were and the couple have been together now for several years.

Anne's story 2

On the other side of the Atlantic, Anne (Step Two, see page 83) had been given her partner's email by a co-worker after she had asked for his help to meet a partner. Emailing back and forth helped her to find out more about him and to get to know him. For months the couple didn't have the time to meet up in person. As a result frequent messages were exchanged, followed by telephone calls:

> *John and I began to email each other and then talked on the phone. We didn't meet in person for several months because of the time pressures on both of us. I did not have any expectations of our first meeting for an ice cream although I was hoping that it would lead to something.*

In the months preceding their meeting, Anne and John discovered that they had a lot in common and liked each other. This was a good start. When they finally met they were delighted to find that the chemistry was there too. Anne liked John's looks immediately although it still took time for the relationship to become more serious:

> *I thought he was beautiful. He seemed very kind, comfortable to be around. I didn't think of him in terms of being my future partner at*

the time. I was just excited that he's a teacher too and we'd have lots to talk about.

He was attracted to me and liked the way I affectionately touched his arm. He still remembers exactly what I was wearing that day: a white shirt, blue Capri pants and white sandals. He was in a short-sleeved olive green shirt, jeans with cuffs. Both of us were quite casual.

Despite being very attracted to him I wasn't thinking that we would marry. It was probably three months later when I really fell in love. I met his family and saw how much family meant to him. At the time I had throat problems and needed surgery. John said he'd go with me to the voice therapist and wait for me in the waiting room. Then we'd have dinner together. His support was amazing; he wanted to be near me.

While on the subject of taking it slowly, you certainly know that friendship can blossom into love. If you saw the film *When Harry met Sally* you will remember how the two were friends first and became lovers much, much later. When they finally did sleep together it was a disaster with regrets all round. Fortunately and with the help of their friends they finally got together and finished the movie happily married.

Christina's story
Like Harry and Sally, Christina and Klaus began their relationship as friends. They met on the Internet and talked a few times on the phone before they met.

I liked his manners and his sophisticated vocabulary over the phone. He stood out from the profiles I had received because he was more intelligent and gentle. When we met, I liked his appearance although I did not like the hippy way he dressed, in particular the male jewellery he was wearing.

Brazilian Christina decided that there was more that she liked than didn't like. After all, most people will make an effort with their clothes and jewellery for their partner.

Our relationship developed gradually. When we met I was interested in someone else. We met as friends, discussing our relationships. I used him as a confidant. One day I told him I could do palm reading and took his hand. He was so moved by my touch that there were tears in his eyes. Something happened between us with that touch that drew us closer.

From the Internet to friendship to romance and a relationship, Christina and Klaus took it in slow stages, and are together 14 years later.

Research confirms that couples that have built their relationship over time have a better chance of success. Think of Kate Middleton and Prince William's eight years together contrasted with Prince Charles and Lady Diana Spencer's whirlwind romance a generation before. Certainly none of the couples whose case histories you have discovered would disagree, whether the couple met face-to-face or on line. All took their time.

2. Face-to-face

Some encounters start off badly. There can be active dislike or just indifference. But this doesn't mean that something more meaningful isn't in the offing. Willow (Step One, see page 45) from Charlottesville met Gage at a meeting of young professionals when she'd just moved to the Southern Town. Their first meeting was not auspicious.

I didn't show up on that guy's radar at all. It was a nothing meeting, he didn't want to stay and talk to me. I didn't care either. We were indifferent to each other. He was polite but clearly wanted to get to the bar.

They both had other thoughts on their mind and meeting a new partner was not one of them. Fortunately they had friends and acquaintances in common and kept bumping into each other.

A couple of months after we met he saw me across the room and this time he noticed me. I was upset and he apparently thought to himself that he needed to help me. He sent me an email to ask if everything was ok. I thought that was sweet. From then on we kept running into each other at business events. We talked more and started to like each other. He asked me out and I said "No" as I was dating someone else. Someone who was not right for me as it turned out and that Gage disliked. He expressed real concern about me several times, not in an all-knowing way, but with genuine caring. He was very persistent and kept asking me out and I kept saying no because of the other guy. Finally we went out twice together. Although I didn't really feel attracted to him I agreed we could remain friends.

It was after that second date that I had what I call my epiphany, I realized that it was Gage that I wanted and that I had been wasting my time elsewhere. I called him and he came over at once and told me he loved me. His goal was marriage, he saw me as marriage material. It took me a week or two before I was hooked. This time it was different from other relationships which were "let's get to know each other and see what happens". The commitment was there, something I had never known before. Gage had been married for18 years, although he was not happy at the end of his marriage. He had been divorced for five years when we met and had dated other women during that time.

So why did it take so long? With hindsight, Willow felt that she had to acquire a certain level of maturity to recognise the potential in Gage instead of carrying on with her "going nowhere" relationship.

We're all at different maturity levels, and we all have different psychological issues. If you meet someone who is looking for a mate, ask yourself what is inside you that needs to change to make it work.

Before Gage came into my life I knew I would meet someone one day. I had a lot of time where I worked on myself. Finally something changed in my body chemistry. I had such a big shift in the type of man I should be with.

Stephany's story

Stephany from Washington DC also did not hit it off immediately with her future husband, Peter, 13 years her senior and divorced with a grown up daughter. They met at a dinner party organised by his sister. She thought he was trying too hard:

Peter loved his work as a journalist. He was gregarious, alive and engaging with a real zest for life that I hadn't come across before. I was flattered that he was so taken with me but I didn't like that he'd had too much to drink which I considered to be a sign of immaturity. He wanted to hire a limo to take me to a business meeting the next morning. I didn't feel I knew him well enough to accept such an offer. I later discovered that he was living with someone.

Although his sister told me things weren't going well for the couple I wasn't interested till it was over. I didn't encourage him yet he kept circling back to me.

Some months later Peter and Stephany bumped into each other at the airport. Both were travelling to different destinations but managed to squeeze in 45 minutes of conversation together before their flights were announced. For Stephany this accidental meeting was like a cosmic message, as if they were meant to meet, as was their third meeting:

I was on a business trip and Peter was on assignment in the same city. His sister got us together over brunch. It was at the time of the

Atlanta Olympics and friends had invited me to stay. Peter loved sports so I suggested he join me at my friends' place. I thought it would be fun to get to know him but that was all. After that he invited me to Aspen for Memorial Day weekend. I decided to plan a business trip to the area and wound up visiting him. It was on that visit that our relationship took off. As luck would have it, I had been interviewing for jobs and the one that came up was in San Francisco, where Peter lived. A cosmic message yet again.

I knew at that brunch, the third time we met, that this was it. I was ready to get married; I even knew what I wanted my wedding dress to look like. He thought it sounded beautiful and asked me about having kids. I said I wanted kids, it was very important to me.

Stephany married Peter three years after they first met. They have twin daughters.

Nathalie's story 2

American writer, teacher and dancer, Nathalie (Step One, see page 55) met her Italian partner, Giovanni, at graduate school just when she had given up on meeting anyone new. Their first encounter, arranged by a friend, took place behind a door.

My graduate school roommate said, "I have someone I think you should meet who is as unique in his own way as you are unique in yours."

I was intrigued, but he was an engineer and rode a bike, like my most recent long-term break-up, so I said, "Nope. Done that. Been there. Never again."

My roommate, bless her heart, said, "Maybe the second time is the charm."

I hid in my room when he came over but I heard his voice at the door and thought, Oh heck, maybe my roommate is correct. I came out of my room to meet him. We talked for three hours that evening, talked the next day, went on a date the next, and there you are. Here was my kind of man. Communication, very few hassles, and lots and lots of fun.

Nathalie was studying, which you have seen is a good place to meet a partner, and she was not afraid to let her close friend know that she had been hurt, which also paid dividends. Plus she was prepared to take a chance and give it another try, in spite of Giovanni's resemblance to her ex.

Here is a case where an Internet meeting would probably not have worked. Nathalie would have taken one look at his profile and discarded it for being too close to that of her ex.

I loved the joy in him. I realized I'd seen him at a Youssou N'dour concert at the university two nights earlier. At that concert, I thought to myself, there is a person full of spirit. He looks like the most spiritual person here. That's something, because we both went to graduate school at a Catholic university, the University of Notre Dame! When I came out of my bedroom to meet him I recognized him.

What made Nathalie so sure that Giovanni was right for her this time?

The difference between Giovanni and my previous partners was how well he listened and remembered what I told him. Also, we agreed almost immediately not to be cruel to each other, to fight fair. We've done pretty well with that one. We made "to be kind to each other" part of our marriage vows.

I realized very quickly that Giovanni and I were beyond good with and for each other. We met in November and I realized by March. At six months, I was ready to marry. It took him a little longer to be ready for marriage—that's probably part of our age difference, too, as well as the fact that in Italy people tend to wait a while before marriage. It's a cultural thing. He told me he didn't even want to consider it before we'd known each other for at least two years. I sobbed and sobbed. But I'm really proud of how present we were with each other in the beginning and how we still are today.

Could the relationship have worked if the couple had met earlier?

We have often talked about this because he is ten years younger than me so this question is even more loaded for us. If I was thirty, and he was twenty, would the relationship have worked? We doubt it. Ten years between us now seems more enriching than it would then, I think. But we both had relationships right before this one that were too long, too mean, and too frustrating, so we wish we had met sooner to avoid those relationships! But my mom says maybe that previous relationship kept me out of circulation, so that I was available and willing when Giovanni and I met. I hope that is true.

Now I'm so grateful that relationship failed. I'm so grateful I came out of my bedroom to meet Giovanni. And I'm so grateful to my roommate!

Nathalie regrets wasting time on a previous relationship, as does Giovanni, showing that you can stay in the wrong relationship too long at any age. Today the two are happy commuting back and forth across the Atlantic.

Give it a chance

The above case histories led to stable relationships even if they didn't start out as such. They have certain points in common which are worth remembering:

- All were prepared to find love, even if they didn't initially think that the answer lay with the person they were meeting.
- All were open-minded and optimistic.
- All took care with their appearance, implying a positive attitude.
- All looked beyond first appearances, and even an initial dislike or indifference, to the spirit within the person.
- All had an inner shift or change, a gut feeling that this time was the right time.

What was different this time?

"For the first time I wanted to make him happy instead of worrying about myself," said Jane when asked how she had realized that she had met her partner. She was in her late 40s and had lived through years of unhappy relationships. In their 60s now, the couple have just got married.

You might also feel more caring than usual. Maybe your attitude is different, or the realization that this relationship makes you happy, or just the fact that everything seems to fit into place. Whatever it is, don't ignore those positive feelings.

On the other hand if there are niggling doubts don't ignore those either. You will look at those later in this chapter.

Exercise 1

A strategy can help you to get to know each other better during your first and subsequent meetings, and get you off on the right footing. It can also help you to become more aware of your own behaviour:

1. It seems obvious but focus on the person you are with. Listen to what they have to say and give them your whole attention. You will learn more about them that way. Live in the moment. Besides, everyone likes to be listened to.
2. Communicate your wishes and desires and make sure that they are heard and understood. Make sure that you don't get stuck in old behaviours. Make it crystal clear what you want.
3. Be brave and honest as you communicate with your new partner. Don't pretend you like something that you don't like or put up with something that isn't for you. It is harder to correct misunderstandings the longer you let them fester.
4. Encourage your partner if it seems appropriate. Don't be afraid to say what you feel even if it doesn't come naturally to you at first.

Compatibility in the first few months: if you clicked it could be wrong

If those first dates went reasonably well it's time to move on to the next stage. By now you've spent some time together and initial prognostics look good. You've probably known each other a few months. All is going well.

Attention: warning signs

This is when the Central Crisis has raised its head in the past. Is this person right for you? Is this someone you could spend time with, even develop a permanent relationship? You identified the values that you want to find in a partner in Step One, as well as those you were hoping not to find. You know that caring, kindness and shared values are important for a couple and some of this seems to be there. Yet you are still not sure. This is understandable, as you saw in the case histories; rare are the people who fall in love at first sight.

Trouble is, you might be feeling that you have had too many beginnings that failed to blossom into anything permanent, that ended around the three month mark. This is because up to three months the couple is *fusional* in their behaviour, almost intertwined. It is later on that cracks start to show.

Thank goodness those cracks do appear; however much you enjoy each other's company, you cannot live permanently joined at the hip. You both need your space and independence. However, if your relationships always break up around the three-month mark, often to your surprise, it could be that you are unaware that you attract partners who can't make you happy. Put another way, their attachment style is not compatible with yours.

In Steps One and Two, you began to remove obstacles that had been blocking you, limiting beliefs that you had imposed on yourself. In Step Three, you will learn about your attachment style, your way of bonding, inherent to you. It is a useful insight to have and one that can become a source of strength once you are aware of it.

Psychologist John Bowlby developed this ground-breaking theory over 50 years ago. It is based on the assertion that humans depend on close relationships to survive. This need is embedded in our genes and is necessary for the survival of the species. It goes right back to the earliest humans who relied upon the protection of their group to survive.

Since then, humans have been programmed to single out a few specific individuals, or attachment figures, in their lives and keep them close. The need to attach is so important that the brain has a biological mechanism specifically for handling the connection to those nearest and dearest. It is called the attachment system and consists of emotions and behaviours concerned with closeness, or distance, from others. While all humans have the same need to bond, the way they go about it can be different.

Attachment theory is a vast and complex body of work covering infant and adult attachment. The following section covers only romantic attachment. (You will find more information in the bibliography).

Attachment Styles: Secure and Insecure

There are two styles of attachment or bonding: secure and insecure. The insecure style has two main sub-groups: avoidant and anxious.

To understand how these styles or behaviours have developed, you need to imagine yourself as a caveman, living in a highly dangerous environment. You can fall prey to wild animals, other humans and natural disasters. You have few means to defend yourself. For you, it makes sense not to get attached to one person. You need to be ready to move on without impediment. You tend to avoid ties too as they hold you back. This is the avoidant attachment style, a person who avoids attaching to others.

Alternatively in this same harsh environment, hyper vigilance and close proximity to your attachment figure might prove more effective. This is called the anxious attachment style as this person needs to attach closely and becomes anxious when the other is not in sight.

Both the avoidant and the anxious attachment styles developed because of the need to ensure protection from harm. If you were lucky enough to be born into a more peaceful environment, you would have the time to concentrate and invest in your attachment figures without fear of unknown dangers lurking behind the bushes. This secure behaviour would yield great benefits for both you and your offspring later. It is called the secure attachment style.

Researchers thought initially that adult attachment styles were a product of upbringing. That is to say that how you behave towards your partner is determined by how you were cared for as an infant and how you responded to your carers. Today this early relationship is considered to be only one of the factors at play.

Understanding why you react in a certain way, thanks to an understanding of your attachment style, can help you to determine whether the people you are meeting can fill your needs. It can help you to use your instincts in your favour instead of against you.

Exercise 2

As you have seen, attachment theory proposes two styles: secure and insecure. It will be helpful to you to identify your attachment style. Your responses to the following questions will give you an idea of which category corresponds best to you. Circle the number of the question that best reflects your current thinking with your new partner:

1. I often worry that my partner will not always love me.
2. I find it easy to be affectionate with my partner.
3. I'm afraid that once my partner gets to know me they'll go off me.
4. I am not at ease sharing my innermost feelings with my partner.
5. Sometimes I feel angry or annoyed with my partner without knowing why.
6. I tend to feel affection for a new partner very quickly.
7. I am generally satisfied with my relationships.

If you felt that questions 1, 3 and 6 come close to your current thinking, you could be anxiously attached. You have the capacity and the need to be very close to your partner. Your relationship is very important to you and you are sensitive to your partner's thoughts and wishes. You might even be a little too sensitive which can make you do and say things you later regret. You need a partner who can provide you with plenty of security in order for you to blossom. You might find yourself constantly guessing what your partner is thinking. That "Why hasn't he phoned?" behaviour of teenagers is typical of the still anxious. Some 20% of people fall into this category.

If you answered true to questions 2 and 7 you are probably securely attached. Relationships come easily to you. You are good at communicating your needs and able to be there for your partner. You are able to sidestep many of the pitfalls that can attract the insecurely attached. Lucky you. This group makes up more than 50% of people.

If you answered true to questions 4 and 5, you are probably avoidant. Your independence is vital and you can be on high alert if your partner shows signs of stepping beyond the borders of what is acceptable to you. Although you want closeness you are not able to open up easily to a partner and of course this can make you very attractive, in particular with the anxious style who will want to come to your rescue. If you feel that your fear of intimacy has kept you from finding your partner till your 40s and beyond, that you are always chasing a new goal, determined not to let anyone too close, even though you really want to, you could fit this category.

Many, although by no means all, humanitarian workers, expatriates and workaholics, fit this group. Note that lots succeed in forming stable relationships and beginning families in their 40s. Being avoidant does not mean that you can't find stability with the right partner. But you will need to learn how to deactivate your avoidant behaviours when they begin.

This is an introduction to attachment style. If you would like to know more about your adult attachment style, you can take an on-line self-evaluation test. Amongst the best are those developed by F Chris Fraley, a specialist in adult attachment theory, see http://internal.psychology.illinois.edu/~rcfraley/

Knowing your own attachment style will be useful to you in all your relationships. You might find that you are insecurely attached with a partner and securely attached with your mother for example.

To really make this theory useful, you need to have an idea of the attachment style of your potential partner. This is the trickier part of the equation.

When you get to know each other better, you could ask him/her to take the self-evaluation test as you did but obviously not immediately. Meanwhile, here are a few pointers that can help you to understand more. Keep in mind that it is harder to identify someone else's style than your own – you don't know them as well as you know yourself, for one thing. You might be overlooking some aspects and giving too much importance to others. Look at the three groups below and see which of them comes closest to your partner.

These exercises are inspired by Dr Amir Levine and Rachel Heller's excellent book, "Attached".

Exercise 3

Group A

- Your partner is negative about some of your behaviours, possibly those that they originally liked about you.
- Your partner appears to have a rigid view of relationships. For example, they always go out with the same type of person, keep looking for "The One" without envisaging other possibilities. They might make sweeping generalizations such as "all men/women want is such and such."
- Your partner doesn't finish an argument by discussing it with you. They blow up and storm out.
- They leave you guessing as to their real intentions and feelings (this can be attractive to the anxious).
- They can't or won't talk about what's going on between you.

Total _____

Group B

- Your partner is reliable and consistent.
- The two of you make decisions together. You are not presented with a fait accompli.
- They have a flexible view of relationships.
- They are open to discussion and compromise.
- They are able to communicate about relationship issues, not take stands.
- You feel comfortable together.

Total _____

Group C

- Your partner wants a lot of closeness, physical contact. You've just met yet there is already talk of mini-breaks and even moving in together.
- Your partner talks a lot about their insecurities. They ask about your previous partners and fear you will leave them. They try hard to please often ignoring their own needs in favour of yours.
- Your partner plays games like not being available on a particular evening just to keep your interest alive.
- They are suspicious that you might be unfaithful to them.

Total _____

Tot up your scores. A maximum of A and your partner could be avoidant, B and you have found a secure partner, C and your partner could be anxious.

Now compare the results with what you know of your own attachment style. Maybe your attachment style is anxious. What will you feel if you meet someone who is avoidant and doesn't want to get too close? Is this going to be the right partner for you? How could you make things easier for each other?

In addition, look out for signs as to whether the partner wants to be close and intimate with you. If they don't and you do, you are not going to get very far with this relationship.

Observe how enthusiastic your new partner is about being with you. Are they too keen, too pushy or just right?

Look at how they communicate. You will look at effective communications in more detail in Step Four. In the meanwhile make sure that you are genuinely expressing your wishes to your partner. Don't be shy about saying you like something or want something else. Better to find out early on than when it is too late.

By the way, statistics reveal that there tend to be more avoidant types in the dating pool than there are in the population at large. Why? Because they are more likely to finish relationships quickly, as soon as the issue of closeness comes up. As they don't attach they get over their relationships quicker and are able to start dating again quicker too.

Exercise 4

It is possible that many if not all of your previous relationships were with people that fell into a particular attachment group. Take this next exercise to see if that is the case. Begin by thinking of some of the first meetings that you have had with previous partners or with those that never got past the first date. Under their name, list your answers to the following questions:

- What was your date's behaviour like on your first meeting?
- What emotions, thoughts, and feelings does it arouse in you today?
- What were the similarities that you notice between these meetings?
- What was different in each case?
- How did they work out?

Do you recognise any of the attachment groups you identified above in your previous partners? Now look at your list of five essential qualities. How many of these showed up in your first meeting? Perhaps one of the qualities you are looking for is reliability but your first date arrives late for no apparent reason. Did you ask them why? Did you explain that this is an issue for you? Your partner might not recognize that there is a problem. If you are able to talk it over you can correct it, particularly when you explain how much it upsets you.

Exercise 5

You might find it helpful to do this next exercise with your partner. Begin by looking at the secure behaviours listed below. When you have reviewed them, discuss your own behaviours and whether they match up with these.

- You are reliable and consistent. You both know where you stand with each other.
- You make decisions together; they are not taken unilaterally.
- You hold a flexible view of relationships and what you are looking for, rather than a rigid view.
- You communicate about your relationship with ease, exploring issues together.

Don't worry if it doesn't match up immediately; it does get easier after 40. When it is right everything seems to flow. It's different to anything you experienced in the past.

Brad's story

American Brad met his Dutch partner Hugo in a gay bathhouse in New York City. He thinks that his use of the law of attraction brought him to this relationship. He was immediately taken with the attraction, charm and sensitivity of Hugo although he had met others in the past with the same attributes.

It was mutual infatuation at first sight. I began to think this was it when on his first return visit to me he expressed interest in meeting my 104-year-old grandmother for whom I was primary caregiver. I initially assumed he would not be interested in hauling a very old lady around the neighbourhood in a wheel chair. Instead, she charmed him, and he charmed her.

Hugo's kindness and interest did the trick for late 50s Brad. He feels that their eleven-year relationship would not have worked had they met when they were younger... Plus they had a continent between them.

The space question comes up again for Brad. You will look at it in more depth, this time from the couple point of view, in Step Four.

Exercise 6

By now you have a clearer idea of where you want to go with this relationship. Nevertheless, it is hard to know in the beginning if it's worth pursuing, particularly if you have a history of getting involved with the wrong person. To help you, here are three questions that you could ask yourself, inspired by Arielle Ford, author of *The Soulmate Secret* who married over 40:

1. Do you feel safe, both emotionally and physically, with this person? You have to answer "Yes" to this question. If you don't, this isn't it. Safety is the most important ingredient in a long-term, happy relationship.
2. Does this person match up with the big five qualities that you listed in Step One? Do you have four out of five matches or none at all?
3. Is this person open, willing and available for a long-term, honest relationship? Are they still locked into a past relationship or caught up with past baggage? There is more about past baggage syndrome in Step Four. How ready is this person to support your long-term goal of happiness? If you are too low on their list of priorities this is not for you unless you like being walked all over.
4. Look at their values. Do you share the same dreams? Do you communicate well, feel compatible, and have good chemistry?

How does it look? If all your answers are positive: congratulations. Just because past relationships didn't work doesn't mean they never will.

Some years back the novels and films about *Bridget Jones* and the TV serial, *Sex and the City*, portrayed the trials and tribulations of the single life for women in their 30s. Could it be that the 40s and beyond are finally the time for a stable relationship for those who didn't settle in their 20s? It seems likely. You know yourself better, understand what you are looking for, and are more able to communicate your needs and compromise.

Becoming more mature explains why marrying in your 40s can give you a better chance at stability. Of course it is not as simple as that or all the unattached would settle down as they hit 40, which is far from the case.

Penny's story

Marrying young is certainly no guarantee of a lasting relationship. Penny, a humanitarian worker, tells how she gets together every year with a group of former childhood friends who had all been to kindergarten together. For years she was the only singleton, all her friends having settled down early on, while she travelled the world. The tables were turned when she married at 50. Suddenly she found herself to be the only one married; all her childhood friends had separated in the meanwhile.

Exercise 7

If you would like to try one more exercise to see if your new relationship is for you, this one looks at what you have in common. This is not for the first meetings, but will be useful when you have known each other around three months. It is similar to exercise 6 but goes a bit deeper. Answer yes or no to the following questions:

1. Does your relationship have trust, respect, loyalty, honesty and commitment? To take it further, you will need to have those essential building blocks to future happiness.
2. How is the contact between you? Do you get the telephone calls, texts, or email answers you want when you want them? Do you like to get an answer back immediately but your partner seems to be in no hurry?
3. Do you enjoy each other's company? Do you have fun together; look forward to seeing each other? If you have the feeling that things are getting a little stale, see what you can do to add a bit of punch.
4. Similar to the previous point, is your partner one of the people you most look forward to seeing? He or she needs to be in your top three at the very least.
5. How exciting is your relationship? Do you feel all warm and fuzzy when you know you will see each other?
6. How do you deal with relationship problems when they arise? You will look at more of these in Step Four.

How did you do? If you got 4-6 it's looking good. Less? You might need to reassess.

Look at the attachment exercises again then move on to facing the challenges of Step Four when you are ready.

In Step Three you explored the Central Crisis. You looked at:

- The first few meetings and how they differed depending on whether you met in person or on the Internet.
- You learnt to give it a chance. If it didn't work immediately it could still change for the better.
- You looked at whether you were compatible in terms of attachment behaviour, comparing your past behaviours.
- You looked at characteristics of the securely attached and the insecurely attached.

Step Four:
Serious Challenges

By the time you reach Step Four you are serious about each other and want to go further. However, there are still some nagging issues in the back of your mind. In this Step, you will encounter a non-exhaustive list of challenges that you could have to face before you decide to commit. Now is the time to address them.

- *Past baggage syndrome*
- *The space question, again*
- *When marriage is the only option*
- *Communications*
- *Children and stepchildren*
- *Age, religion, education and culture*
- *Finances*

"It takes a lot of courage to show your dreams to someone else."
Erma Bombeck

You have succeeded in reaching Step Four: congratulations. You have cleared away many of the obstacles that had blocked you in the past, met someone new and decided that there is potential for the two of you to go further. So far so good. Life can still throw you a few more challenges on your way to committing to each other.

The situations that you will be facing are different to those that you would have faced 20 years ago. You have more experience of life, are clearer about what you will accept and what you won't. You have your own way of doing things. Over the years, you have had good and bad relationships. Many have left their mark on you emotionally.

As a result, you have a different perspective today at 40+. Nevertheless, younger and older couples do have one point in common: during the infatuation stage, they tend to skate over their problems, thinking that it will all change once they are married. It won't. Now is the time to face worries and concerns so that you are aware of their potential to harm your relationship. You don't want them springing up to surprise you in a few years' time when routine has set in and you are less forgiving of your partner's weaknesses.

This Step is illustrated with examples of couples who did face difficult circumstances, some of them extreme. Bravely and honestly they reveal how they have come through situations that could have driven them apart. They also share how they found a way of dealing with them. All the couples went on to commit and are sharing their lives together today.

Past baggage syndrome

The first challenge, and arguably the most common, is past-baggage syndrome; what each of you brings to your relationship in terms of unresolved conflicts. In the survey for this book, 50% of respondents found their own issues had repercussions on their couple while 62% were affected by their partner's concerns. Past baggage is almost a given for a couple marrying later. But it is up to you how big a place you are going to allow it to have in your relationship.

Elizabeth's story

Elizabeth and Richard met and married in their mid-50s. For her, it was her first marriage, for him his third. They enjoy each other's company, travelling and exploring. They have recently upped and changed countries and now plan to move again. Life is an adventure and the world their oyster now that children have grown up. Nevertheless, both had childhoods and life experiences that were painful. They show considerable courage in sharing. Elizabeth says:

I had a difficult childhood as my father used to beat me and send me to my room with no food or drink for hours on end. I have never understood why I was singled out - I have four siblings - but by the time I was 12 years old, my whole family had turned against me and I found myself ostracized with no one to turn to. My schoolwork suffered and as a consequence I was denied the opportunity to go to university. This has always been a source of great frustration for me. The treatment I received means that, to this day, I have difficulty expressing myself and forming opinions (I would always be told to 'shut up').

Her father's behaviour towards her also influenced her choice of partner.

As is so often the case, I sought out (unknowingly) and found a man who would also beat me and put me down. The aggression only started when my daughter was born, but it was so bad that I had to obtain a restraining order against him. He dragged me through the courts for ten years, demanding access to the child he couldn't care less about and, although I won the case, it left me feeling very low. After that abusive experience, I thought I was so emotionally challenged that I would never find myself in a loving relationship again. I was to be proved wrong, but I needed masses of trust and respect to overcome my fear.

Elizabeth has her own way of dealing with her past, and Richard's understanding is vital to her:

My past does come back to haunt me quite regularly as if it's on a constant loop. I never had answers to any of my questions regarding the treatment I received. Both of my parents have passed on now, so I'm not likely to. I keep searching for hidden clues in the recesses of my mind. I want to try to make sense of it all and finally put it to rest. I feel blessed that I've found someone who takes the trouble to try to understand and who is better-placed than most to deal with the frustration that wells up when those memories surface and I need to vent my anger. Richard and I are able to share those moments together and are all the stronger for it. Age helps too. We mellow and unhappy experiences of the far-distant past lose their hold little by little.

Richard also had a difficult time as a child although in a different way to Elizabeth, as she explains:

Richard had had a somewhat traumatic childhood as his parents divorced when he was 6 years old (which was unusual in the late 1950s and made him 'different' from other boys). His mother brought him back to the UK from Singapore where his father was stationed and they had to live with relatives until his mother was able to find work. The divorce was rather acrimonious and he and his sister were caught in the middle. As he had no father figure in his formative years, he rebelled as a teenager and his schoolwork suffered which meant that he never had the opportunity to go to university which, in turn, meant that he had to struggle to make a living.

At the time of our meeting, Richard told me that he was in a relationship and that he had been married and divorced more than once before. I have to admit that this rang a few alarm bells. I subsequently realized that his upbringing had had such a huge impact on him that, in his quest for the stability he had never experienced, he had rushed into inappropriate relationships. They never lasted.

Richard and I experienced different events in our respective childhoods. Nevertheless, we come from very similar social and cultural backgrounds and therefore have a deep understanding of each other's makeup and what makes us tick, for want of a better expression. Richard doesn't allow his past to encroach upon the present.

Couple relationships are often founded on conscious and unconscious recognition of experiences and knowledge that the two hold in common. Issues like those faced by Richard and Elizabeth require a good deal of understanding on the part of the partner. With patience and understanding this couple is overcoming past baggage syndrome to live a happy and stable present.

Exercise 1

This exercise is designed for both of you to do together. It concerns questions to ask when the past keeps coming up and one or other of you is having difficulty putting it to rest. Recognize though that no one has a completely clean slate, particularly as the years go by.

1. What does focusing on the past do to us?
2. Is it helpful or a hindrance?
3. Do I have a right to judge my partner?
4. Am I letting bad feelings about my partner's past relationships influence me?

Look at your answers and ask yourself honestly if the issues you are concerned about are acceptable or too overwhelming for you to come to terms with. The idea that "After we are married, it will all be different" is a myth. Now is the time to address problems.

Exercise 2

This is another exercise for the two of you to do together. The past will always be there, it has helped you to become who you are. It is only when it keeps creeping and interfering in your present that there is a problem. If you find yourselves continuously concerned with your past, it is time to define a new standard for the relationship, to make a new plan for your life *à deux* and commit it to as a couple. Both of you need to be in agreement.

1. In the best of all possible worlds, how would you like your relationship to be?
2. Where is it going?
3. What is acceptable for you and what is not?

The space question, again

As you learnt in Step One, the amount of space you need has its origins in childhood and in culture. What is more, now, at 40+ you are used to having your own space, and probably your own home. You come and go as you please, leave your belongings where they fall, don't mind whether the fridge is empty or full. Now, all of a sudden, you are thinking very seriously about moving in with your partner. Even with the best of intentions, this can prove to be a challenge. In Step One, you looked at making space to attract a new partner into your life. You did well and now that partner is here and is or will be sharing your space. How comfortable do you feel about it? Do you wish you could keep your own home and have your partner too?

For many 40+ couples that would be idyllic: your partner and your own home. You could meet up at weekends and special occasions but keep the status quo, you each would have your own space to be alone when you need to be. Many dual-career couples have accepted living in different countries as a way of life and often maintain that living that way helps keep the relationship fresh and new.

Couples where one partner travels to exotic places often claim to have the best of all worlds. Often at the beginning of the relationship they can accompany their partner into unchartered territory. Then, when they have been together a while, the partner might travel alone. They have the home to themselves during the partner's absence. In both cases they are creating an adventure within the confines of routine, they are rekindling excitement when they need it most.

Christina's story 2

Christina (Step Three, see page 107) and Klaus are married yet they live 50 miles apart. The advantages and disadvantages of their arrangement have changed over time. In their early 40s when they met on the Internet, they were together for four years before deciding the time was right to marry. During those four years, Christina took the courageous step of suggesting couples' therapy to assess their readiness for marriage:

> We went to a therapist together on my initiative to be sure we were ready for marriage. We went for two years. It was a chance to get to know each other better, see potential areas of difficulties. I was scared of commitment and wanted to minimize the risk. For me, marriage was scary. Partnership you can get out of, marriage is more serious.

When the couple decided to marry, they kept their own flats while Klaus looked for a new place that both could share. Christina continues:

> Neither of us had ever lived with anyone so it seemed natural. After we married, Klaus began looking for a bigger place for us to share, between where we both lived but nearer to him. Professionally it would have been easier for Klaus than for me to move. The tight housing market meant that it took him a year to find a suitable home, large enough for both of us to share. When he finally found a flat, I changed my mind and proposed we continued to live in our own homes. He didn't object and so we continued to live in our own homes.

The couple has now celebrated their 10th wedding anniversary together. They meet up at weekends and special occasions and talk a lot on the phone. Nevertheless Christina would like more intimacy at this stage in their relationship:

> By not living together, keeping our own flats, we minimized the level of adaptation required. We were able to stay in our comfort zones. With hindsight, I think that it is important to step out of your comfort zone. Living together is a sign of real intimacy and real commitment. In some ways, it is against Christian values to live apart. We are committed but not as much as couples that live

together. We live parallel lives; meeting to share weekends and holidays. Now we are used to it and Klaus cannot imagine changing.

I think that our arrangement works because our relationship is not that passionate. It is more intellectual and emotional than physical. I have noticed that other couples who live apart, for example, in different countries, are more like friends than lovers. The friendship element is very strong.

In addition to their friendship, there is considerable commitment on both sides; the couple has been together for 14 years.

Phoebe's story

Living apart doesn't work for everyone. Phoebe decided she needed to meet the challenge of living with her partner. In her mid-40s, Phoebe rented a cosy little one-bedroom flat where she felt comfortable and secure when she met James, a divorced father of two. Phoebe's split-level flat had everything she needed and was within walking distance of the office. Plus it was not expensive. She was sorely tempted to keep it on when she and James decided to rent a house together:

Happily I didn't. I am sure that had I kept my flat the relationship would not have gone ahead. Every disagreement or situation that I didn't like would have sent me scurrying back to my own space on the other side of town. By taking the decision to move in with my partner, I proved to myself that I was prepared to give it a try.

Phoebe has now been with her husband for over 15 years thereby proving that her decision was the right one for her. These last two case histories have in common that both couples decided to look for a new flat to begin their couple life together. They did not want one partner moving into the other's home. This is a sound approach to dealing with the space question. However happy you are in your old home it has ghosts or at the least it is marked by your personal tastes and habits. It will not be easy for your partner to fit in and feel totally committed to the space. You will both be more comfortable somewhere new, in a home that is neutral to you both, if your circumstances permit.

Exercise 3

Sharing your space can easily lead to conflict. You need to be prepared to deal with this and other issues that will arise. Even if you rarely argue now, conflicts come up for everyone. This exercise gives questions for you and your partner to ask each other about this sensitive issue.

1. How did your family solve conflicts?
2. When do you use the same style that your family used?
3. What do you think works with this style of conflict solving?
4. What doesn't work?

Review your answers with your partner. They will help you to prepare for the inevitable arguments.

When marriage is the only option

For some couples, their relationship is put to the test too early on by the Authorities. Tough immigration laws in some countries mean that they are forced to commit to marriage, like it or not, when they want to live together but are of different nationalities. At the end of her best-selling memoir, *Eat, Pray, Love,* American author Elizabeth Gilbert fell in love with a Brazilian-born Australian. Both had survived difficult divorces and didn't want to remarry. However, fate intervened; they were forced by the US authorities to marry if they wanted to live in the US together. Gilbert tackled her fears of marriage in her book *Committed, A sceptic makes peace with marriage,* by delving whole-heartedly into the topic, trying to understand what the institution of marriage was all about. As she explains:

> *Our resistance to marriage, then, had nothing to do with an absence of love. On the contrary, Felipe and I loved each other unreservedly. We were happy to make all sorts of promises to stay together faithfully forever. (…) The problem was that the two of us were survivors of bad divorces, and we'd been so badly gutted by our experiences that the very idea of legal marriage – with anyone, even with such nice people as each other – filled us with a heavy sense of dread.*

Reluctance to marry can come from experiencing an ugly divorce. The separation and loss can be your own or that of your parents when you were a child. Overcoming the fear and learning to trust can take half a lifetime or maybe more to achieve, but it can be done with patience and understanding.

Alexandra's story

Alexandra had lived through the second case scenario, the painful divorce of her parents when she was only five. Suddenly in her late 40s she had to face her reluctance to marry the man she loved. The law in her adopted country gave her no choice; it was marriage or living an ocean apart.

The couple met when Alexandra took a trip to Cuba with eight friends from her Salsa dancing class. To get a real Salsa experience, the class would dance with local Cuban dance partners. One of these was Carlos. The two hit it off very quickly. Carlos was genuine and didn't seem to be trying to impress, unlike men she had met before:

> *I was attracted to people who were not bound by limitations, who were authentic. Carlos is macho but has no issue with me being strong.*

Alexandra met Carlos in March. In June she decided to return to Cuba:

> *I've never been back to the same place so quickly and on top of it to see a guy. I didn't think we'd marry or live together but definitely wanted to give it a try. I went back in October for 10 days and then December for a month, travelling around the island. The following year I returned three times for two-week holidays. We toured extensively together, often going on trips to the coast. One evening we were having a beautiful dinner just the two of us when he said we'd be together for a lifetime. I thought it could be an option, but he said he didn't want to leave Cuba. I replied that I couldn't stay so we dropped the subject.*

It was natural that Alexandra would also like Carlos to visit her adopted country. She had not expected to be faced with a visa problem:

> *I tried to get him a tourist visa, but the Authorities denied my request as they were afraid he would stay. I spent quite a lot of money on legal advice. When I appealed, the Authorities again said that they had no guarantee he would return to Cuba. I then tried to get him an invitation to come to my country, Germany, to create a*

workshop with the opera house. The German embassy also denied my request saying they had no guarantee Carlos would leave when his work was finished.

As the relationship took shape, Alexandra got stubborn; she wasn't going to let a faceless power decide about her happiness.

I discovered that there was a visa for foreigners who intend to get married which is valid for six months. It still took nearly a year to get the documents and involved time and even bribery money in Cuba. When we finally got the visa we discovered it was only valid for three months, such was the local rule.

We got Carlos's exit permit on July 23. He arrived on July 27 with a visa that was due to expire on August 24. The migration office agreed to extend if we'd produce a wedding date. However, when we went to the Town Hall we were told he couldn't marry once the visa expired. They gave us an ultimatum: either marry now or he has to go home.

The final straw came when the Town Hall told us we needed a translator. How could I get someone in a few hours? I broke down. I felt attacked, like there was no help, everything was difficult, nobody cares, nobody helps. I blanked out my emotions and put on my battle suit. Carlos and I were in this together. I separated my love for him from the battle I was fighting.

Alexandra was sure of her love for Carlos, but still had nagging doubts about having to get married:

It was tough for me to be forced into marriage. My parents' marriage fell apart when I was five, which was why I had been reluctant to commit earlier in my life. In fact I didn't think I'd get married, I had never found a partner to have children with so I didn't think I needed to marry. But with Carlos I couldn't do much else if we wanted to live together, which we did.

The impact when marriage came up was powerful; on the one hand I wanted to think I was marrying for purely administrative reasons but then other stuff came up, like the fact that marriage is for a long time. I don't know why that is. If it's just for administrative reasons why do romantic images come into play? I was experiencing two perspectives. I wanted to have a party because marriage is special but is it special?

Elizabeth Gilbert explains the need human beings have to be in a couple:

A lot of people, as it turns out, want intimacy with one special person. And since there is no such thing as intimacy without privacy, people tend to push back very hard against anybody or anything that interferes with the simple desire to be left alone with a loved one. (...) We just keep insisting on the right to link ourselves up to another soul legally, emotionally, physically, materially. We just keep on trying, again and again, no matter how ill-advised it may be.

Alexandra and Carlos married without the benefit of living together, discovering each other daily and letting their love grow. Nevertheless with patience it is working out for them.

Communications

No matter how keen you are to be together, couple attachments present challenges, as well as opportunities, to all who seek them.

Victoria's story

Victoria and Manuel have been together two years now. From very different cultures, they face difficulties in their day-to-day lives in addition to those that all new couples have. Manuel has moved to Austria, Victoria's country and has had to integrate, firstly by learning the language. Victoria says:

Communication is a big one, as a coach I work hard on this. Manuel doesn't like to talk conflict. It is difficult for him to accept I'm not attacking him directly. I'm proud to say what's bothering me yet he feels attacked and attacks back. Then I feel shit this didn't work at all. Sometimes I tell him it bothers me if he doesn't bring up the topic.

One of their communications issues is about sharing her flat. As you saw earlier it is preferable to take somewhere new, however in this case it was not possible:

We are living in my flat so he feels he doesn't own anything. But he doesn't say that to me, I heard it through friends that he'd spoken to. He doesn't want to tell me what he wants. I assure him that I need him to speak to me but instead of being a friendly conversation of needs it becomes a blaming conversation. I don't want to go there. I feel frustrated, here I am a trained professional communicator and it doesn't work at home.

So how does she deal with it? Over time, Victoria has developed a strategy:

Showing vulnerability, emotions, asking him for input, instead of providing solutions. When I share what I don't know, it works sometimes.

It's not second nature for Victoria who is 10 years older than her partner, but she is starting to see that her strategy is paying off.

Like this couple, you and your partner could be at different stages in your emotional development. Perhaps one of you finds it difficult to heal and be reconciled, for example, when communication is blocked by pain and lack of forgiveness. Or you might fear taking the risk of being vulnerable to your partner, or like Manuel have a need to avoid conflict. Adjusting to each other's sets of needs and styles can be a challenge.

FOCCUS, Inc. USA offers a Pre-Marriage Inventory known as FOCCUS, Facilitating Open Couple Communication, Understanding and Study. Certified facilitators located on 6 continents and 38 countries currently use the FOCCUS Inventory. Over the 30+ years of offering FOCCUS to engaged couples of all ages, communication and problem solving skills have been determined to be important factors in how couples work through issues in their marriage.

Each person in the couple responds to a series of nearly 200 statements in various topic areas and their individual responses generate a personalized Couple Report. A trained facilitator then meets with them to facilitate couple exploration of the topic areas. Through discussion, reflection and ongoing attention to these topics areas, couples become more skilled and confident in their ability both individually and as a couple, to address whatever issues arise in their marriage.

Based on what FOCCUS and others in the field of marriage education realize regarding the importance of strong couple communication and problem solving skills, I have developed exercises for you to use according to your goals and the needs of your own relationship.

Do the next two exercises together. They are helpful in developing listening and communication skills. Sit back, relax and enjoy them.

Exercise 4

Do you feel that your partner is a good listener?

1. If so, why?
2. If not, why not?
3. What are the family listening behaviours that each of you was brought up with?
4. When do you feel that your partner is listening to you (give examples)?
5. When do you feel that they are not listening to you (give examples)?

Exercise 5

Do you feel that you can express yourself clearly to your partner?

1. Does your partner like to communicate with you on all subjects?
2. Are there subjects that they do not like to discuss, which ones?
3. Are there circumstances where communication is more difficult?
4. If so where and what would help?
5. What would make communication better between you?
6. Can you establish a plan and if so how would it look?

Exercise 6

Finally, here is an exercise on feeling good together. How relaxed do you feel around your partner?

1. In what circumstances do you feel most relaxed together?
2. When do you feel least relaxed (This can be spoken or non-verbal)?
3. Can you recognise when your partner is feeling relaxed?
4. How can you promote more togetherness?

When the couple communicates well together they can establish what works and what doesn't early on.

Paul's story

Paul was single, in his late 40s when he met Susanne online. He appreciated her laying down the communications ground rules in their relationship:

> *From the first everything was perfect, although I couldn't believe it. I was afraid I wasn't seeing the real person, only the projections of my imagination on her. I'm a bit introverted and reserved and I'm not so good at talking about my thoughts, wishes, feelings and emotions. It was a relief to me when she told me that I wasn't responsible for her life and she wasn't for mine.*
>
> *I needed to adapt to spending most of our free time together. I had so much less time with my colleagues and for myself. There were several little things that I changed, that weren't so important, so I could do them easily. One such was having no television in the household.*

They are the same nationality and lived near each other before they met. Their opinions about culture, children, parents, pets, finances and shared space were similar.

> *Our ideas and opinions were very similar or almost the same. I was more afraid about my weaknesses and faults. So I try to correct and improve them and to see my wife in difficult moments like I saw her the first time when I fell in love with her.*

Paul looks back on his past relationships and realises that differences of opinion are necessary, but in small things:

> *I think the aims, wishes and dream for our relationship and life, together, the main topics, should be similar. For example if I want to live in town and she hates towns and wants to live in the countryside, it'll be very difficult for us to come together. In small things, it's interesting and supporting to be different and to complement each other. I guess that, in my successful partnerships, we were similar*

in the main things and different in the small ones, and in my unsuc-cessful ones we were different in the main things and similar in our weaknesses so we couldn't complement and support each other.

As you saw in Step One, you have issues that are negotiable and issues that are non-negotiable. Perhaps, like Paul's example, living in the town rather than the countryside is one of them. Questions like these need to be addressed before you marry for you both to be satisfied with your arrangement. One of your non-negotiables could be children.

Children and stepchildren

Most of the couples interviewed claimed that they never really wanted children; it was not an issue. If you really want children and no long-term relationship would be complete for you without them, you need to make it clear from the outset.

Susanne's story 3

Susanne (Steps One and Three, see pages 49 and 105) hasn't had children and does have regrets:

I had always wanted to be(come) a mother, preferably of at least three children ...

If I could turn back time, I would have started to look more actively for a potential husband and father at a younger age. Most importantly, I would have declared that I wished to get married and have children, rather than to believe well-intentioned advice that you scare men away if you dare mention any of this. If this is the case, then be glad of it, because they would clearly have been the wrong ones to help you realize your heartfelt wish and lifelong dream.

By the time I was forty, I had tried online dating, after attempting many other avenues. It was still something relatively new. I stated my wish for marriage and children of my own in my profile straight away – so as not to waste any precious time with men who either still hadn't made up their mind in that respect or who didn't want children.

You looked at the essential qualities you expected from a partner in Step One. Once again, if having children is one of your essentials, make sure it is on your list.

Giancarlo's story 2

You might be happy with your choice of a partner, but it's possible that your family has doubts. Giancarlo (Step Two, see page 96) was in his mid-50s when he married his long-term partner. His mother was not happy that his bride was older than him:

My mother wanted grandchildren. I am an only child. I also miss having children, but I think I put it off for so long because of the easy life we led in the 70s. We got into the habit of not taking responsibility. I did think about having children in my 40s but by that time it seemed too late. I don't think it's a good idea to have them when you are too old.

Many contemporaries of Giancarlo who came of age in the 70s and never married nor had children say the same thing. It was a time of new freedoms and many didn't want to accept commitment. Many did though.

Stephany's story 2

Without children yourself, you might find a partner who does have one or more children from previous relationships. This can be a tricky issue, irrespective of their age. Says Stephany (Step Three, see page 110) about her grown up stepdaughter:

His daughter didn't want us to marry nor have children. This was a real challenge and one we didn't overcome. Once we had children she was so angry.

It all comes down to communications again. Your partner's child was there first and a bond has already been created that you are not part of. It takes a special understanding and consideration from your partner to allow you to take your own place. Many parents feel guilty about the break-up of their marriage and their feelings are complicated. Be clear on what you expect and remember that time is the biggest healer. This is a very difficult hurdle to cross and one that many couples don't succeed in dealing with. Yet it needn't destroy the couple.

Eleanor's story

Early 50s Tim had a young daughter. His guilt about the break-up of his marriage had led him to spoil her. His new partner, Eleanor, had not been married before and was not used to children. She was overwhelmed by the amount of space the child was allowed to take:

> Some couples have alternate weekends with their children. This was not our case. Tim would keep his daughter for weeks on end and then not see her at all for weeks. I also think that his ex-wife would make things difficult. She would insist Tim pick up their daughter at 7 in the morning on a holiday Monday for example.

Eleanor tried all sorts of approaches to make things work. Tim wanted the three to be a family, going on outings together. Eleanor didn't feel that was her role. She suggested to Tim that he and his daughter see each other for dinner regularly, without her. This gave her time to herself and allowed the father-daughter to spend time together.

Exercise 7

This exercise gives sample questions for you and your partner to ask each other about your children from a previous relationship. Discuss with your partner some of the changes your marriage will bring into your lives in terms of the children:

1. What changes do you expect?
2. Have you discussed them with your children?
3. Together?
4. Alone?
5. Is a family conference a good format for you?
6. What changes do the children expect?
7. What do they fear?

Exercise 8

Here are some questions to help you and your partner to determine the role that your children will have after you marry:

1. What might be appropriate times for the children to come first?
2. Do you both agree?
3. Does either of you see the other as unreasonable in this matter?
4. What will happen to the couple relationship if the children usually/always come first?
5. How was this worked out in your previous marriage if you were married before?
6. Have you shared with your children any change they can expect in their relationship with you? What to expect?
7. Are the children willing to include the new spouse into the family unit?
8. How will this happen?
9. What ways can you find to help it happen?

Age, religion, education and culture
Beverley's story 2

Beverley (Step One, see page 60) married a younger man. In her opinion, she faced four challenges to her marriage: age, religion, education and culture. Of these, only religion remains an issue for the pair who have been married near to 20 years.

I would love him to take an interest in the Bible, to join study classes with me. But I made the choice to be with him and have to keep praying. Maybe in time God will change his heart. I try not to push him. He agreed to come to church with me for about five years, but that has stopped since I changed churches and it's no longer practical.

The differences in age and education have had positive repercussions on the couple:

The age difference pressures me into staying as young as I can, it's challenging. I used to get angry when asked if he was my son, but that doesn't happen anymore.

The challenge of education was overcome when we moved to the States. I have a Ph.D. As soon as we moved here from Turkey, he began attending school, got a BA with almost straight As then went on to get his MA. I helped him financially and encouraged him in whatever he wanted to do. He has a job in community college in Colorado where he got his second MA. Now he wants a Ph.D.

While there are differences, it is what unites them that keeps this marriage so strong:

Our values are very similar in most things such as integrity, honesty, doing things right, helping each other out, and family.

We have a poodle, he's our child. Ahmed never dreamed he'd have a dog or that he'd kiss a dog, but he is crazy about this one. He would have made a good father although he would have spoiled the children rotten.

It would have been easy to say that the differences between Beverley and Ahmed were too numerous, that it would never work. And yet it has, spectacularly.

If you are facing challenges of this sort it could be helpful to look at Beverley's example and consider what holds you together, what binds you and how you can draw the positive out of your differences. For example do you have a big age difference? It can help keep you young.

Finances

Money issues are known to be right up there amongst the principal causes of divorce for first marriages. They are high on the list of destructive factors for second marriages too. Couples need to examine their communication and problem-solving skills in working through these conflicts and come to a compromise or acceptance before marriage.

In addition to the challenges mentioned above, Beverley feels that money, or what to do with it, keeps the couple on their toes:

I'm more of a spender, he is a saver. Our values were different although they are closer now. Money was always hard for him to get in childhood, but not for me. I used to collect when I was in Europe for the day when I'd get married. In the beginning, it was hard for me to share with another person. I'm conscious of it.

Exercise 9

There are many questions that you and your partner need to ask each other about this touchy subject. At 40+ when you probably each have your own incomes, these will not be the same as for 20+ couples starting out in life. Nevertheless financial issues should not be overlooked. Here are some questions to help you check for possible disagreements:

1. What financial decisions will be made jointly and which will remain separate?
2. What concerns do you have about money?
3. How do you both like to spend money and to save it?
4. Who will handle the paying of bills, how and when?
5. How and when will you discuss the status of the account?

In addition to establishing how much is available and for what, you also need to decide on the methodology you will use as raised in questions 4 and 5 above. You might like to sit down once a week, for example, on Saturday mornings, to plan for the week ahead. This would be the time for you to pay the bills jointly. You can also check your agendas so that one of you hasn't invited the other to an event on an evening when they are busy. Discuss what you will be to doing next week and on which days. It is important that both of you feel involved in everything that concerns the couple. If one partner does the payments, for example, even if the money is provided by both, the other partner needs to feel involved in the decision process.

This Step has been a challenge in itself. You have looked at some painful issues and seen how others have dealt with them. You have also done exercises that will help you to communicate and problem-solve more clearly. You are taking with you that no matter how different you are, discussion, communications and problem-solving will stand you in good stead for the future. As will shared values.

Congratulations. When you are ready it is time to take the last Step, the one that leads you to say "I do."

In Step Four you looked at:

- **What each of you brought to the marriage in terms of old baggage and how to deal with it. When it's too much and when to let go.**
- **Different solutions to the space question.**
- **Couples who have had to commit for legal reasons.**
- **Improving your communications and problem-solving skills.**
- **The question of children, yours and theirs.**
- **Differences of age, religion, education and culture.**
- **The prickly problem of finances.**

Step Five:
Final Union and Fulfilment

When you picked up this book you were at home feeling lonely. Then you heard The Call. You went Outside into the World and had some Initial Success. You dealt with the Central Crisis and overcame the Serious Challenges that life threw your way. You have now reached the fifth step in your journey to marriage over 40: Final Union and Fulfilment. In this Step you decide on whether to go further and to prepare for your new life together.

At last you emerge victorious to lay claim to the treasure, the kingdom, and your Hero.

In Step Five you will discover:

- *First time marriage over 40: A good idea?*
- *Any regrets?*
- *The long-term objective*
- *Why marry?*
- *The meaning of the ceremony*

"Of all the souls that stand create
I have elected one." Emily Dickenson

First time marriage over 40: A good idea?

When you have been single on and off for around 20 adult years, finding yourself in a committed relationship will require you to adapt. Of course you love your partner, but that is not the whole picture. Are you ready to take that leap and make that change?

To help you to take your decision, the couples in this book share what they think are the advantages of marrying over 40 and what they enjoy about married life. The answers are beautiful and inspiring.

The positive side of marriage over 40 is that you have had the time to explore, develop, do many of the things you wanted to do, before settling down. Most of the major developmental changes affecting your private and professional life occur between 25 and 40. This is the reason that couples who marry young with plenty in common often feel that there is little between them by the time they reach their 40s and have taken different paths. Both have grown in different directions. For you that is good news. With those years behind you, you will find it easier to grow with your partner at this stage in your lives.

Alfred, married at 50, says that:

I'm much happier now than I've ever been although marriage takes work every day, it's not easy. There were good times being single. By waiting longer I was able to finish my Ph.D., start a profes-sional career and travel a lot which I couldn't have done married. My life has been atypical. Not many people have had the luxury of visiting 60 different countries through work, had relationships with girls from different cultures. I've brought something away from each of those relationships. All of this has made a difference in how I see the world. It has matured me, made me more culturally aware in a good way.

Willow echoes Alfred when she says:

I feel grateful I found someone but also grateful I had 20 years single as an adult to do all the things I wanted. I've had the best of both worlds. If you don't have a strong desire to be a parent you are not missing anything by marrying later.

There is something about making a firm commitment, in writing, signed and counter-signed, that frees you to invest. Silke had been putting money aside for years to buy property. Only trouble was she couldn't decide where she wanted to live:

I was torn between the town where I lived, where I wasn't all that happy, and buying a studio in the mountains for the holidays. The reasoning behind it was that even if I changed towns I would always be happy to come back to my studio for the holidays. Only trouble was I don't really like the mountains, I much prefer the sea. I went back and forth with friends to look at mountain homes but never really found what I was looking for.

All this changed when she got married in her mid-40s:

We lived in the same town although neither of us was born here. We didn't have any reason to move. It seemed logical to put my savings into buying a house for the two of us.

The couple have since sold their first house and bought a flat with the proceeds. They are still no nearer to finding a holiday home but enjoy having the freedom to explore new places.

Before marriage Kevin had avoided getting a mortgage because he thought that it would box him in, like marriage. His reasons for committing in his early 40s were partly practical:

We have joint ownership of our house if one dies. Marriage also gives me legal rights over the children. I wanted to get married, to show that we are a couple and I am committing myself, to make a public declaration. Now it is clear on the forms.

The relationship developed over a year and a half before the couple decided to buy their house. Kevin admits that he has had to adapt to marriage and make adjustments:

Now I have to take my wife's view into account. I have to check with her if I want to meet someone else for a drink. There are practicalities like that.

After many years as a bachelor, Kevin considers spending time just the two of them to be essential, especially in the evenings.

> *The kids stay with their father often so we have time to ourselves. We enjoy being together. We do simple things like watching television, it's valuable down time.*

The idea of investing, constructing, building something together is also present for Giancarlo:

> *I married at 56 after many years of living together to formalise the relationship and to give it a more serious aspect for my partner's children, our friends and families as well as greater security for her. Marriage gives stability, it is something more consequent than living together. It also convinced us it was time to invest. We bought a flat in the south of France which we wouldn't have done otherwise.*
>
> *Yes I'm pleased I married. The fact of being married is reassuring. It gives you a companion, a partner. Marrying someone older, more mature, gives me security. I'd like to have more time for us to share, to do things together, to talk. We are also business partners and I think that being married has helped us professionally.*
>
> *I regret not having taken the decision sooner but it just didn't happen because I hadn't met the right person. I wanted to be different, not average.*
>
> *Marriage is like building a house. When you marry you lay down the foundations for your new home. Carefully you put each brick into place, making sure the base is as solid as possible. But you do not construct the whole house in the first months or years together. It takes time, year after year to build a structure that you are comfortable and happy to live in.*

Frank also uses the analogy of building something together through commitment:

Marriage has given me a huge stability. Finally I have a life partner, someone to count on, all those things that I didn't think were important before I married. I have no regrets.

We felt like we were made for each other. We could stay committed. This is what I was looking for, someone to spend time with but who would also let me do my own thing. We have a good business partnership too as Renée is more financially analytical than I am. We have investments together and run some seminars jointly, we also have real estate investments.

The first steps you will probably take are those that transport you from your own home to a life with your new partner. Diplomat's daughter Nilufar was used to travelling during her childhood, leaving homes and countries often. Nevertheless leaving her home for marriage was a bigger step:

When I married I was frightened at the idea of leaving the nest, of the transition from one security blanket to another. Marriage has taught me tolerance. I accept things that I would not have accepted before. I am no longer able to just please myself and listen to music at 4 in the morning. I have to think of someone else. It is scary after all these years of independence... and I'm fed up with cooking dinners.

I know it is not easy to find the right partner. I have found the right person in James who supports and loves me. He is not a womanizer and I can trust him. He is a good match for me. As for regrets, ask me in 10 years time. Sure there are things we would both like to change about the other - but hey - comes with the territory - we just deal with it. It is so nice to have a wonderful person to share your days and nights with whatever the age you get married.

You will need patience and compromise to adapt to another person's habits and behaviours, but it should be worth it. Beverley can't imagine life without Ahmed:

He is an excellent cook, much better than me, but he often leaves a mess in the kitchen. When I start to get cross with him I think it's silly to get annoyed about small things when he gives me so much. The majority of time we get along pretty well, and we plan on being together for a long, long time.

He took out a big insurance policy and jokily told me how I could get my hands on all that money, but I pray for his safety every day, I don't want anything to happen to him. He's healthier now than he was when I met him as I'm into nutrition.

Any regrets?

You have probably had a number of relationships. Some could have worked and you did spend a while together. Others couldn't, yet you still spent a while together. One of the commonest regrets from couples is about the time they wasted on the wrong person. You can't get that time back but you can draw the line, realizing that it was thanks to those other people that you learnt some lessons and became the lovable person you are today. They shaped you into who you are and helped you to understand who you aren't. Often the insecurely attached can recognise the moment they were ready to move towards a more secure attachment by the person they were with just before they met the partner that finally won their heart.

Karin's choice of Sven as a boyfriend was not a good one; he was bankrupt following a disastrous business deal. On top of it, there was no chemistry between them. On the plus side Sven was kind, reliable and always there for Karin.

In the past her relationships had been with men she couldn't count on because of her own fear of being tied down.

Spending time with divorced Sven did prepare me for real commitment even if there were other problems. He was reliable, unlike his predecessors. By accepting that someone could be there for me, I opened the door to my future husband.

Anne is happy living as a couple. She wishes she had known it would be this good instead of wasting valuable time with the wrong person:

I was in a long-term relationship before I married. Although I knew I wasn't going to marry him I stayed because I loved him, I would not have stayed that long if I'd realized how much better things could be.

Anne and her husband invest time and energy into making their marriage work.

My shirt says 'Plan your marriage BEFORE you plan your wedding' and that is a maxim that I follow. John and I go every year to at least one conference about marriage to stimulate us. We started teaching a marriage enrichment class which we found very helpful for our own marriage. John is so supportive of the institution; he understands the importance of working on our marriage.

At one point we worked in John Gottman's research laboratory. Our job was to watch videotapes of couples having disagreements. We had to see if they kept using the five signs of stress which Gottman has identified including interrupting each other and stonewalling. John and I took his workshop in Seattle.

I'm proud of our shirts. Mine says 'I love my husband' and his says 'I love my wife'. He wears his shirt as his pyjamas. Just to see him wear it makes me feel so good. Often he's on his computer and puts on our wedding song 'Broken Road' and I go rub his back. He makes me feel incredibly loved.

They don't have cultural differences but they do have an eight-year age difference, Anne says:

It means I need to exercise to keep up with him, nothing more at this stage.

Marriage has also brought her the happiness of a new family:

> *When you marry someone, you marry his family. His mum is like my new best friend. I've always adored his family since I first knew them. They live an hour away, and I love to visit them.*

A new family is an added bonus for many older couples, in particular those who come from smaller or dysfunctional families. Says Christina of the new family she cherishes:

> *Marriage has given us a sense of togetherness, of commitment. It has also given us a sense of family. I don't have much family anymore and so I feel connected to his, they are my adopted family.*

Nathalie with her younger Italian husband who she met at university is very happy with her marriage but like Anne regrets time wasted:

> *Our marriage is the best thing I've ever done. No regrets in terms of our marriage. But I do regret all the time I wasted on relationships that were painful and unsupportive and unnecessary. People say you grow and you learn from those kinds of relationships, but from my perspective now—being with my husband—those earlier relationships just feel like a massive waste of time. I regret how I used to worry about relationships that were patently absurd. I used to hang in there with relationships like a little terrier, never letting go. Some bones should just be buried, so you can move onward.*

The surviving partner of the only couple in this book that are not still together, Stephany, regrets that she didn't meet Peter sooner. They knew each other for three years before they married. Only three and a half years into their marriage her husband fell ill and subsequently died. She remembers the good things that they shared:

I liked having a partner, a built-in best friend. I enjoyed taking care of someone and having the security and comfort of growing together. I loved being able to share our children's experiences, growth and wonder with him. We motivated each other, our intimacy was wonderful.

Stephany decided on a religious wedding to mark the importance of the event in her life and to keep with traditions:

I decided it was important for me because I hadn't been married before. I wanted to have children and as I'm traditional I didn't want them out of wedlock. We had a Jewish ceremony for me although he didn't convert. Peter didn't care about organised religion. In the Jewish tradition the groom treads on glass signifying a new beginning and putting the past in the past. That was significant for me.

The long-term objective

Alexandra has not let her husband's visa problems upset her first experience of living with him:

I like living together, it's the first time I've lived with someone. There is a question of commitment once you are married, an intention to make it work, a longer-term objective.

I feel held, like I belong to somebody. He's my home. What I liked and fell for in Cuba is here too. He added something to my life. I am totally in love with him. I am curious to know what is our outlook. Of course we can't look into the future. My mother, who was not happy about our relationship initially, is now at peace with it. She used to be concerned about what would happen in 10 years time. Her friends said that if our marriage lasts 10 years that's more than most. It will last the time it will last.

Marriage is a long-term investment. It has to be taken one step at a time, built up brick by brick. Each new day, month and year is a milestone to be celebrated for what it has achieved.

For Consuelo who found love in Brooklyn, marriage is a blessing:

> *Marriage means having a person that you plan with, do things with, support and help each other and have fun with. Hopefully as you grow older you will live together and take care of each other. In a marriage, each person should naturally put the other person first. When you do this it is a daily blessing of love and care and happiness.*

She takes a positive view of her single life as she moves on to this new stage:

> *I don't miss anything about being single but I didn't dislike it. It was a wonderful part of my life. Everything about being together is just a joy and comfort. I'm so blessed and so grateful. No regrets.*

Elizabeth loves laughing with her partner and:

> *The companionship. The cuddles. The sharing. The emotional security. His wacky sense of humour (with a squiggly red underline). Always having someone to play Scrabble with and to cook for (and knowing it will always be appreciated!). Having a back to warm my icy toes on. Cups of tea in bed in the morning. The way he always wants me to be happy. Who could ask for anything more?*

Like Consuelo, she can appreciate the good side of marrying later:

> *There are advantages to marrying over 40: The fact that you've both done all the crazy things by then (well - most, one would hope) and you're more emotionally mature. If there are children, they have most probably flown the nest, so you have the time and space to appreciate each other all the better.*

Paul had been in a long relationship before he met Susanne online. His previous partner died before they could marry:

It's marvellous to have somebody who loves me and who I love, who attracts me and is attracted by me, it's beautiful to share the good things and moments, and the bad ones too, to undertake things together, to help each other in daily life and in attaining our dreams, to have my wife as my safe haven.

All these can be in a relationship too, but being married is stronger and deeper. The existence of our union is shared in public with our relatives, friends, even with the places we visit.

His wife Susanne agrees:

It's wonderful to know that we belong together, to share life as husband and wife, to face the challenges of life together and to cherish and celebrate its joys. I love to be there for Paul, to care for him, to love him, to encourage him, to comfort him, to tease and to challenge him. I know I can trust him completely. I would do (almost) anything for him – and so would he for me. Thanks to him and his love I can achieve goals I thought were way beyond me. We try to encourage each other to realize our own dreams as well as our common wishes. We share many interests and views and often think the same thing at the same moment.

Marrying Paul has been the best thing I've done in my life so far. I would gladly do it all over again! I wish I had met him earlier, although I'm not sure that I would have been ready for him then.

Marriage does take a loving relationship to another level. It's no guarantee it will last. It's an obligation to take special care and responsibility to make it work and to keep growing together as well as individually. We can't succeed alone, that's why we ask God and the community for their blessing and support.

You have read what others think about married life, do you feel that this commitment is for you now, at this time? Here are some questions that will shed light on your feelings, and those of your partner, around this important decision.

Exercise 1

Doubting whether your commitment will last a lifetime is a perfectly normal fear to have, in particular if you have had several relationships in the past that didn't last. Perhaps you are wondering what is different this time. These questions can be answered with your partner:

- What are your fears and concerns about making a life commitment?
- Can you talk about these together?
- Do you have the same or parallel fears and concerns?
- How can you provide each other with assurance and comfort?
- What does it take to commit for a lifetime?

Exercise 2

You need to consider the many changes that marriage will bring your way. You have looked at some of these. Here are some questions to help you explore further:

- What kind of lifestyle changes have you planned together?
- What kind of lifestyle changes could happen that you have not considered?
- What can you do to make the path a smoother one?
- How will you both continue to help each other in the future?
- Do you have any non-negotiables about what you can/ cannot accept in terms of change?

Why marry?

At 40+ it is unlikely that you will be forced into marriage, unless you face immigration laws such as those discussed in Step Four. And yet the institution of marriage remains extremely popular, one that the couples you have met in this book all felt was important to them.

Why marry you might ask, rather than live together? No one will frown upon you if you don't officially tie the knot and yet the institution survives, albeit in a different capacity to that of our parents and grandparents.

Jessica considers herself to be traditional and old-fashioned:

Marriage feels nice, secure. It is more solid, making a commitment. We have spent two wonderful years together. I have learned things about myself, maybe I wasn't ready before.

The role of marriage has changed dramatically in the last 50 years. The rapid growth in later and same sex marriages shows that its purpose is no longer primarily as a base for bringing up a family. While the rigid rules and regulations of our parents' marriages are no longer adhered to, expectations have risen; marriage has become a partnership intended to provide a safe haven in a changing world. The expectations placed upon it are not the same as they used to be. In some ways they are higher, although it is easier to escape if things don't go right. Some years ago there was a worrying US trend whereby couples divorced not because they weren't happy together but because they expected more if they stayed together. Because marriage is entered into voluntarily today, we often place expectations upon it that are beyond its scope.

Exercise 3

If you are secretly hoping that marriage will solve some of the major problems in your life, it is time to do the following exercise:

- What problems are you hoping that marriage will solve?
- How can you solve these problems independent of marriage?
- If these problems could be solved in another way, is marriage still a priority for you?
- How will these problems affect your relationship if you do decide to marry?
- What are the short and long-term consequences?

The meaning of the ceremony

It is so important to have an official ceremony, a culmination of all that has gone before. You have read quotes from couples who married over 40 on the previous pages and what they feel about being married. All decided to make a public declaration.

What is it about a public, legal marriage that means so much to everyone, anyhow?

Asks Elizabeth Gilbert in her book when debating her own reasons for remarrying.

Ceremony is essential to humans: It's a circle that we draw around important events to separate the momentous from the ordinary. And ritual is a sort of magical safety harness that guides us from one stage of our lives into the next, making sure we don't stumble or lose ourselves along the way. Ceremony and ritual march us carefully right through the center of our deepest fears about change.

The real importance of this ceremony is so that everyone knows where they stand in relation to everyone else, who they are. No more embarrassing introductions of my er, um, partner. Suddenly his sister becomes your sister-in-law, your mother is her mother-in-law; everyone is squared away and can get on with the business of living.

When my sister married, I pondered what I was going to say. The couple had been living together for eight years, what was the meaning of marriage to them today? It was simple really; in the eyes of God, their families and friends, the two were making the public declaration that they had chosen each other. They were about to take their vows and spend their lives together. And by so doing they were confirming to the rest of us where they stood and where we stood. They could move on with their lives, on to the next chapter, married life.

In Step Five you looked at:

- First time marriage over 40 and whether it is a good idea for you.
- What others regretted, or not, about marrying later.
- The long-term objective of marrying later.
- Why marry and whether it will solve other problems.
- What the ceremony means to you and to others.

Afterword

I don't regret marrying later, although it wasn't easy being single that long either. There were so many things that I wanted to do, places to go, things to explore, before I could commit. I broke off past engagements because I wasn't able to give up my space or freedom that easily. I was lonely sometimes, but I had to go through those times. They allowed me to grow.

One thought kept me going throughout my single years: the unshakeable belief that I would meet someone one day and it would be for the rest of my life. I never wavered, no matter how low I felt.

Had I married younger, some things would have been different; I would probably have had children although I'm not certain, I would have known my mother-in-law for longer and both my husband and I could have known our fathers-in-law. Younger, we would perhaps have built more bridges together, but again I'm not sure.

It wasn't to be. I believe that there is a time for everything. My childhood traumas had to take time to heal; I had to learn to trust.

Throughout this book I have insisted that to be over 40 and single is not a matter of being left on the shelf. It's not like a child that fails to make the first selection for the netball team. On the contrary, the single person holds themselves back from settling down through their own personal issues. They could have been caused by trauma, relocation or commitment to studies and career. Whatever the reasons, it doesn't really matter anymore. What does matter is the damage that they can be doing today. If that is your situation, I hope that this book has helped you to recognize and work on these issues.

Sadly, there is still the view that "you missed the boat" and "it's too late now". Waiters make you feel bad when they ask, "*Are you all alone?*" and give you the table at the back, next to the lavatory.

Shopping for one when supermarkets package for families of six is expensive and isn't designed to meet your needs. Staying in hotels that charge exorbitant rates for single occupancy rooms is not fair. With this book I hope to have reassured you that you haven't missed any boats and it is never too late to meet your partner. I did it, and so did many others who have shared their stories with you. If we can do it, so can you.

Society is starting to pay more attention to later marriages. As people live longer, it is more likely that they will decide to marry later, if at all, or for a second or third time. When I married, I knew few people in my situation, since I have written this book I have discovered that marriage over 40 is more and more usual for the first time and particularly for the second or more time.

When you marry later after years of singledom, you step into a whole new world, a whole new adventure. While others who married young are divorcing, you, the late bloomer, are just getting into your stride. Your pleasures are different over 40 but they are just as rewarding. Challenges too are different and are faced in ways that your younger self could not have imagined.

There is little research available on whether later marriages are more stable. Nor is there much on whether later couples change their attachment style, hopefully from insecure to secure. These are fascinating subjects that I continue to explore.

The stories in this book accurately reflect what has been reported to me by each participant. In order to protect their identity, I have changed the places and the names of all those who kindly responded to my survey.

My story and those of other respondents represent the most common issues which can arise but are not intended to be exhaustive. Similarly the exercises address these common issues but also are not the only ones possible.

When I was single and in my twenties and then thirties, my father used to say,

"Marriage isn't perfect, but it's the best we have."

After more than ten years of married life, I believe that marriage is not only the best we have, but the best way to celebrate and safeguard a loving relationship. I hope that you do too.

Bibliography and further reading

Bowlby, John, *The Making and Breaking of Affectional Bonds*, (Routledge, London, 1979, 2005)

Ford, Arielle, *The Soulmate Secret* (Harper Collins, New York, 2011)

Gawain, Shakti, *Creative Visualization* (A Bantam New Age Book, 1979)

Gilbert, Elizabeth, *Committed, A Sceptic Makes Peace with Marriage* (Bloomsbury Publishing PLC, London, 2010)

Gottman, John, *The Seven Principles for Making Marriage Work* (Three Rivers Press, New York, 1999)

Gottlieb, Lori, *Marry Him, The Case for Settling for Mr. Good Enough* (New American Library, New York, 2011)

Hendrix, Harville, *Getting the Love you Want* (Simon and Shuster, 2001)

Holmes, Jeremy, *John Bowlby and Attachment Theory* (Routledge, 2005)

Edward O. Laumann, John H. Gagnon, Robert T. Michael and Stuart Michaels, *The Social Organisation of Sexuality: Sexual Practices in the United States* (University of Chicago Press, 1994)

Levine, A. and Heller, R., *Attached* (Penguin US, 2010)

Greenberger, Dennis Ph.D., Padesky, Christine, Ph.D., Mind over Mood (The Guilford Press, 1995)

Waldman, Adelle, *The love affairs of Nathaniel P.* (London: William Heinemann, 2013)

Watson, Shane, *How to Meet a Man After Forty, and other midlife dilemmas solved* (Penguin Books, London, 2009)

Whitworth, Laura, Kimsey-House, Karen, Kimsey-House, Henry, Sandahl, Phillip, *Co-Active Coaching, New Skills for Coaching People toward Success* (Davies-Black Publishing, Mountain View, California, 2007)

Additional resources

Marriage preparation
FOCCUS
Facilitating Open Couple Communication, Understanding and Study
https://www.**foccus**inc.com

Attachment self-evaluation
F Chris Fraley
adult attachment self-evaluation
www.psychology.illinois.edu/people/rcfraley

Quotes used in this book can be found at **www.goodreads.com**

About the Author

Lesley Lawson Botez, MSc, is an English-born writer and psychologist. She met her husband in her 40s. She was travelling with friends to the desert. The hows and whys of late marriage raised so many questions for her that she decided to investigate further.

Lawson Botez began her writing career as a copywriter for Saatchi, before setting up her own communications agency. At the same time she was Geneva correspondent for *Swiss News* and contributed articles to the *Financial Times* and *Newsweek* to complement her copywriting. She sold her agency to set up the Communications Department of a private bank and then train and advise on publication concept and production at the International Committee of the Red Cross.

Lawson Botez studied psychology at Webster University and Geneva University. She is qualified in Cognitive Behavioural Therapy and in Co-Active Coaching.

She is completing a Master of Fine Arts in Creative Writing at Kingston University London. She teaches academic English and copywriting at business universities and writing schools.

Lawson Botez was awarded second prize for non-fiction in the Geneva Writers' Group 2014 literary awards. Her first short story, *First Choice*, was published in *Offshoots 12*. Visit her website www.lesleylawsonbotez.com for more information.

She lives in Geneva with her American husband.

Disclaimer

The contents of this book are designed to provide information and to assist the reader to better understand his or her own situation in the light of the experiences of the author and many others. It does not constitute medical nor psychological advice.

Romance, erotica, sensual or downright ballsy. When you
want to escape: whether seeking a passionate fulfilment, a
moment behind the bike sheds, a laugh with a chick-lit or a
how-to – come into the Bedroom and take your pick.
Bedroom readers are open-minded explorers knowing exactly
what they like in their quest for pleasure, delight, thrills or
knowledge.